Department
for Transport

Know Your
TRAFFIC
SIGNS

Official Edition

SITE COPY

700043639716

London: TSO

Department for Transport
Great Minster House
33 Horseferry Road
London SW1P 4DR
Telephone 0300 330 3000
Website www.gov.uk/dft
www.gov.uk/traffic-signs

© Crown copyright 2007, except where otherwise stated

Copyright in the typographical arrangement rests with the Crown.

You may re-use this information (not including logos or third-party material) free of charge in any format or medium, under the terms of the Open Government Licence v3.0. To view this licence, visit www.nationalarchives.gov.uk/doc/open-government-licence/version/3 **OGL** or write to the Information Policy Team, The National Archives, Kew, London TW9 4DU, or e-mail: psi@nationalarchives.gsi.gov.uk

Artwork of traffic signs should be reproduced accurately and not in a misleading context, for example not on roadside billboards.

ISBN 978 0 11 552855 2

First published 1975

Fifth edition 2007

Twenty First impression 2017

Available from www.tsoshop.co.uk

Printed in Great Britain on paper containing at least 75% recycled fibre.

Contents

Introduction

Why know your traffic signs?

Traffic signs play a vital role in directing, informing and controlling road users' behaviour in an effort to make the roads as safe as possible for everyone. This makes a knowledge of traffic signs essential. Not just for new drivers or riders needing to pass their theory test, but for all road users, including experienced professional drivers.

Keeping up to date

We live in times of change. Society, technology and the economy all play their part in changing the way we travel. New road signs conveying new messages and in new formats are introduced from time to time, so drivers or riders who passed their driving test a few years ago need to keep up to date or run the risk of failing to understand or comply with recently introduced signs.

Do you understand the colour coding on signs such as this?

A few examples of events that called for new signs include:

- Britain's first motorway
- Pelican crossings
- Reintroduction of trams
- Advanced stop lines
- Vehicle-activated signs
- Active Traffic Management.

Having experience is all very well, but it's not enough if your knowledge is out of date.

Responsibility for traffic signs

Responsibility for the road network in the UK is split among:

- the Highways Agency in England
- the Welsh Assembly Government in Wales
- the Scottish Executive in Scotland
- and local or regional highway authorities.

The central administrations above are responsible for the UK's strategic road network. Strategic roads are the highways that link cities, areas of population, ports and airports. Most motorways and some "A" roads are strategic roads.

Local or regional highway authorities are responsible for local roads, and this includes a few motorways, all other "A" roads and all other public roads. While responsibility for placing, erecting and maintaining traffic signs is split among these bodies, it is important that signs are consistent both in appearance and in the way they are used.

To ensure that the UK has a uniform traffic signing system, signs must conform to the designs prescribed in the Traffic Signs Regulations and General Directions (although some signs may have been specially authorised by the Secretary of State).

The Traffic Signs Manual, published by TSO, provides detailed guidance for those responsible for designing and installing traffic signs.

For more information about traffic signs guidance, see **www.dft.gov.uk/pgr/roads/tss**

A brief history of traffic signs

It was probably the Romans who first used "traffic signs" in Britain. They marked off road distances at one thousand paces (about one mile) with stones called "milliaries".

Most early signposts were erected by private individuals at their own expense. A law passed in 1648 required each parish to place guide posts at its crossroads, but it was not until after the General Turnpike Act 1773 that these "guide posts" or "fingerposts" became more common.

During the second half of the nineteenth century, bicycles became more popular. Steep hills and sharp bends were very dangerous for early cyclists, and "danger" and "caution" signs were erected at the top of steep hills. Signs showing skull and crossbones were erected at the most dangerous places. Local authorities and cycling organisations installed an estimated 4000 warning signs.

The year 1896 heralded the era of the motor car, and some motoring associations took up the business of placing signs. The Motor Car Act 1903 made local authorities responsible for placing certain warning and prohibitory signs. The signs were for crossroads, steep hills and dangerous bends. "A" and "B" numbering of roads was introduced in 1921, and these numbers were shown on fingerpost-style signs alongside the destination and distance. Town or village name signs and warning signs for schools, level crossings and double bends were introduced at the same time.

The main task of signposting our roads during the 1920s and 1930s still fell on the motoring organisations, but in 1931 a committee chaired by Sir Henry Maybury was asked to recommend improvements to the signing then in use, and by 1933 further new signs began to appear, including "No entry" and "Keep left" signs, warning signs for narrow roads and bridges, low bridges, roundabouts and hospitals. Other signs followed during the 1930s, including "Halt at major road ahead". These formed the basis of our traffic signing until the early 1960s.

It was not until after 1918 that white lines began to appear on British roads, and during the 1920s their use spread rapidly. In 1926 the first Ministry of Transport circular on the subject laid down general principles on the use of white lines. In the 1930s, white lines were used as "stop" lines at road junctions controlled by either police or traffic lights. Reflecting road studs (often referred to as "cat's eyes") first came into use in 1934. By 1944, white lines were also being used to indicate traffic lanes and define the boundary of the main carriageway at entrances to side roads and lay-bys, and in conjunction with "halt" signs. In 1959, regulations came into effect to control overtaking by the use of double white lines.

It was realised that the old system of signing would not be adequate for motorways, and the Anderson Committee was set up in 1958 to consider new designs. It recommended much larger signs, with blue backgrounds. Then, in 1961, the Worboys Committee began to review the complete system of traffic signing. It concluded that the UK should adopt the main principles of the European system, with the message expressed as a symbol within a red triangle (for warning signs) or a red circle (for prohibitions). Work began on the conversion of British signs in 1965, and this is still the basic system in use today.

Later developments include the use of yellow box markings at busy road junctions, special signs and road markings at pedestrian crossings, mini roundabouts and bus lanes. Regulations published in 1994 included new regulatory and warning  signs and simplified the yellow line system of waiting restrictions that was originally introduced in the 1950s. Further Regulations were published in 2002.

More use is being made of new technology to provide better information to drivers on hazards, delays and diversions. The future will undoubtedly see more developments in traffic signing to keep pace with the changing traffic demands on our roads.

The signing system

There are three basic types of traffic sign: signs that give orders, signs that warn and signs that give information. Each type has a different shape. A further guide to the function of a sign is its colour. All triangular signs are red.

Circles
give orders

Triangles
warn

Rectangles
inform

Blue circles generally give a mandatory instruction, such as "turn left", or indicate a route available only to particular classes of traffic, e.g. buses and cycles only

Red rings or circles tell you what you must not do, e.g. you must not exceed 30 mph, no vehicles over the height shown may proceed

Blue rectangles are used for information signs **except** on motorways where blue is used for direction signs

Green rectangles are used for direction signs on primary routes

White rectangles are used for direction signs on non-primary routes, or for plates used in combination with warning and regulatory signs

There are a few exceptions to the shape and colour rules, to give certain signs greater prominence. Examples are the "STOP" and "GIVE WAY" signs

The words "must" or "must not", when used in the descriptions that follow, refer to legal requirements that have to be obeyed.

9

Warning signs

(other than those for low bridges, railway and tramway level crossings, bus and pedal cycle facilities, traffic calming and road works)

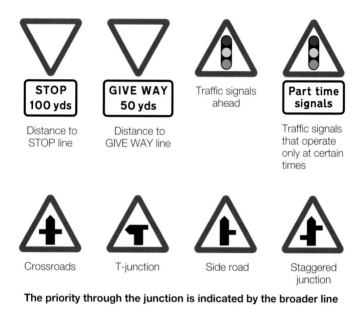

Distance to
STOP line

Distance to
GIVE WAY line

Traffic signals
ahead

Traffic signals
that operate
only at certain
times

Crossroads

T-junction

Side road

Staggered
junction

The priority through the junction is indicated by the broader line

Traffic merges
from the left

Traffic merges
onto main
carriageway

Roundabout

Bend to right
(left if symbol
reversed)

Double bend
first to the left
(right if symbol
reversed)

Junction on a bend
(symbols may be reversed)

Plate used with
"roundabout"
or "bend" signs

Sharp deviation of route to the left (right if chevrons reversed) (alternative designs)

Adverse camber

Risk of lorries overturning on bend to the left (right if symbol reversed)

Block paving incorporated into a roundabout to indicate sharp deviation of route

REDUCE SPEED NOW

Plate used with warning signs where a reduction in speed is necessary

Road narrows on both sides

Road narrows on right (left if symbol reversed)

Plates used with "road narrows" signs

Oncoming vehicles in middle of road

Single file traffic

Single file traffic in each direction

Single track road

Road wide enough for only one line of vehicles

End of dual carriageway

Two-way traffic

Two-way traffic on route crossing ahead

Near-side edge of carriageway or obstruction near that edge (alternative shapes). White markers are used on the off-side edge and amber ones on the off-side edge of a dual carriageway

Worded warning. "Ford" may be varied to "Flood", "Gate", "Gates" or "No smoking"

Try brakes after crossing a ford or before descending a steep hill

Steep hill downwards (10% is equivalent to 1:10)

Steep hill upwards (20% is equivalent to 1:5)

Sign used with "steep hill" or "try your brakes" signs

Low gear for 1½ miles

Low gear now

Keep in low gear

Plates used with "steep hill" signs

Opening or swing bridge

Quayside or river bank

End of bridge parapet, abutment wall, tunnel mouth etc.

Water course alongside road

Soft verges for 2 miles

Soft verges for distance shown

Tunnel

Hump bridge

Uneven road

Slippery road

Side winds

400 yds

Distance to hazard

250 yds ←

Distance and direction to hazard

For 2 miles

Distance over which hazard extends

Low-flying
aircraft or
sudden
aircraft noise

Gliders likely

Low-flying
helicopters
or sudden
helicopter noise

Risk of falling
or fallen rocks

Traffic queues
likely ahead

Slow-moving
military vehicles
likely to be in
or crossing
the road

Slow lorries
for 2 miles

Slow-moving
vehicles for
distance shown

Risk of ice.
"Ice" may
be varied to
"Snowdrifts"

Warning of signals
(see page 120).
"FIRE" may
be varied to
"AMBULANCE"

Other danger. The
plate indicates the
nature of the hazard

Zebra crossing

Pedestrians in road
for distance shown

Frail pedestrians
likely to cross

Disabled
pedestrians.
"Disabled"
may be varied
to "Blind"

School

Children going to
or from school

Patrol

**Disabled
children**

Alternative plates used
with "school" sign

Lights warning of
children likely to be
crossing the road
on their way to or
from school (used
with "school" sign)

**Pedestrians
crossing
200 yards**

Pedestrians likely to be
crossing a high-speed
road where there is no
formal crossing point

Horse-drawn
vehicles likely to
be in the road

Accompanied
horses or ponies
likely to be in or
crossing the road

Wild horses
or ponies

Wild animals

Wild fowl

Migratory
toad crossing

Sheep

Farm traffic

Agricultural
vehicles

**ANIMAL DISEASE
RABIES
INFECTED AREA
AHEAD**

Area infected by
animal disease

Cattle grid with indication of bypass for horse-drawn vehicles and animals

Cattle

Supervised cattle crossing ahead

Supervised cattle crossing

Regulatory signs

(other than those for low bridges, railway and tramway level crossings, bus and pedal cycle facilities and road works)

Most regulatory signs are circular. A **RED RING** or **RED CIRCLE** indicates a prohibition. A **BLUE CIRCLE** generally gives a positive (mandatory) instruction or indicates a route for use only by particular classes of vehicle (see sections on tram signs and bus and cycle signs).

Two notable exceptions are:

The **"STOP"** sign and road markings: you **must** stop before crossing the transverse line on the road and ensure the way is clear before entering the major road.

The **"GIVE WAY"** sign and road markings: you **must** give way to traffic on the major road (the upright sign or both the sign and the triangle on the road might not be used at junctions where there is relatively little traffic).

No entry for vehicular traffic, including pedal cycles (usually indicates the end of a one-way road where all traffic is travelling in the other direction)

No vehicles except pedal cycles being pushed by hand

Alternative plates used with the "no vehicles" sign, indicating times when vehicles are prohibited, except for access

No motor vehicles

No motor vehicles except solo motorcycles

No solo motorcycles

No towed caravans

No pedestrians

No ridden or accompanied horses

No horse-drawn vehicles

No articulated vehicles

No goods vehicles over maximum gross weight shown in tonnes

End of goods vehicles restriction

No vehicles or combinations of vehicles over maximum length shown

No vehicles carrying explosives

17

No vehicles
over maximum
width shown
(width shown
in metric and
imperial units)

No vehicles
over maximum
width shown
(width shown
in imperial
units)

No vehicles over the maximum
gross weight shown in tonnes.
The bottom plate is used where
empty vehicles are exempt

Plates used to indicate exemptions from prohibition signs

Except for access to
premises or land adjacent
to the road, where there is
no other route. Other
exemptions may be shown

Except for loading
and unloading by
goods vehicles

No
overtaking

Where a road or bridge is very
narrow, priority must be given to
traffic from the other direction
(there will usually be a "give way"
line indicating where to wait)

**Where changes of direction are prohibited, a red bar across the
sign is used in addition to the red circle**

No
U-turn

No
right turn

No
left turn

Except
buses and
cycles

Exemption
plate

Vehicles must not go beyond the sign where displayed by a school crossing patrol

Vehicles must not go beyond the sign where displayed by a police officer or traffic warden

Specified traffic must not use verge maintained in mown or ornamental condition

Proceed in direction indicated by the arrow

Turn left ahead (right if symbol is reversed)

Vehicles may pass either side to reach the same destination

Keep left (right if symbol reversed)

Plates supplementing "turn" signs

Mini-roundabout (give way to traffic from the immediate right)

One-way traffic

Nature of and distance to a prohibition, restriction or requirement

Weight restriction ahead (may show a different restriction)

Location of weight restriction ahead with indication of an alternative route (may show a different restriction)

19

Speed limit signs

Remember that in areas of street lighting (other than on motorways) a 30 mph limit applies **unless** another limit is specifically signed.

The maximum speed, in miles per hour, at which traffic may travel, if it is safe to do so

The national speed limit for the type of road and class of traffic applies

A larger sign indicates the start of a speed limit. Smaller repeater signs act as reminders. Repeater signs for a 30 mph limit are used only on roads with no street lighting. Repeater signs for the national speed limit are used only on roads with street lighting (other than motorways)

Road marking used in conjunction with upright signs to indicate the speed limit

Entrance to a zone where a 20 mph speed limit is enforced by traffic calming measures (there may be no 20 mph repeater signs within the zone)

End of 20 mph zone and start of 30 mph speed limit

Start of a speed limit at the boundary of a town or village

Start of motorway regulations, including the national speed limit (unless a different speed limit is signed)

Point on a road with street lighting where an existing 30 mph limit originally ended but has subsequently been extended (temporary sign). This sign alerts drivers that a previous higher limit has been replaced by a 30 mph limit by the removal of speed limit signs

End of road works and any temporary speed limit through those works (may be supplemented by a sign indicating the permanent speed limit beyond the road works)

Area where speed cameras are in use

Length of road where two cameras are used to measure the average speed of a vehicle between two points

Reminder that enforcement cameras are in use (may be supplemented by a speed limit sign)

Speed camera nearby on a lit road with a 30 mph speed limit (i.e. where there are no speed limit repeater signs)

Speed camera nearby on an unlit road subject to the national speed limit (i.e. where there are no speed limit repeater signs)

Maximum speed advised, in miles per hour, at a bend (the plate may be used with other warning signs)

Minimum speed permitted, in miles per hour, unless it is impracticable or unsafe to comply

End of minimum speed requirement

Low bridge signs

Each year there are hundreds of incidents in which bridges are struck by vehicles too high to pass under them. Both rail and road users have been killed in these incidents. Look out for signs in this section and **make sure that you are not a bridge basher**.

All bridges with a clearance of less than 16 feet 6 inches (about 5 metres) are normally signed. Both regulatory roundels and warning triangles can be used, depending on the type of bridge.

Bridges particularly at risk from strikes may have a variable message sign that is activated by high vehicles passing through an infra-red beam. When the sign is activated, four amber lamps flash, the top pair alternating with the bottom pair.

Regulatory signs

No vehicles over the height shown may pass the sign (height shown in metric and imperial units)

No vehicles over the height shown may pass the sign (height shown in imperial units)

At non-arch bridges mandatory signs may be used; it is unlawful for an overheight vehicle to pass one of these. They are placed on the bridge and at the side of the road in front of the bridge.

Advance warning of a mandatory height restriction ahead; the sign may include an arrow, if the restriction is on a side road

Location of mandatory height restriction ahead, with indication of an alternative route

Warning signs

A warning sign indicates, in imperial units, the maximum headroom under a bridge or other overhead obstruction. There may be an additional sign showing the height in metric units. These signs may be sited well in advance of a bridge, with the distance, either in yards or miles, shown on a plate; this may have an arrow to indicate that the bridge is on a side road at a junction ahead.

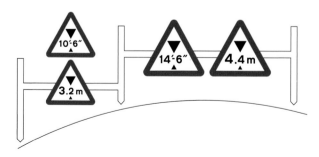

Chord markings used indicate the points between which different headrooms over different parts of an arch bridge are available.

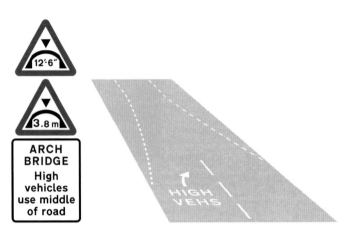

The maximum safe headroom at an arch bridge is shown on the triangular warning signs. Road markings guide high vehicles through the highest part of the arch. Drivers of all vehicles should give way to oncoming high vehicles in the middle of the road when there is insufficient room to pass. Drivers of cars and other low vehicles may keep to the left-hand side of the road, crossing the road markings, where this would enable them to pass oncoming vehicles in safety.

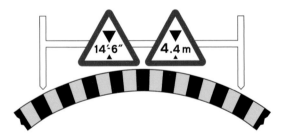

To improve the conspicuity of a bridge, black and yellow bands may be added to the arches or beams and to the abutments.

Where reduced headroom over a road is due to an overhanging building or structure, a plate may be added below the warning triangle to indicate this ("building" may be varied to "buildings" or "structure").

Signs incorporating height restriction roundels and warning triangles

Roundels or warning triangles will sometimes be incorporated into directional signs that may also indicate an alternative route to take to avoid the low bridge.

Roundels may also be incorporated into road works signs to indicate temporary height restrictions.

25

Level crossing signs and signals

Before the crossing

Level crossing with a gate or barrier

Level crossing without a gate or barrier

STOP when lights show

Plate used with level crossing warning signs: advance warning of light signals at a level crossing with or without a gate or barrier

Safe height 16'-6" (5.0 m)

Electrified overhead cable and the safe height beneath it (usually associated with an overhead electrified railway or tramway). On the approach to a junction, the plate may include an arrow to indicate the direction of the level crossing

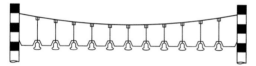

Bells suspended over the road at a railway crossing to give an audible warning to drivers of vehicles that exceed the safe height beneath electrified overhead cables

Drivers of LARGE or SLOW VEHICLES must phone and get permission to cross

LARGE means over 61'-6" (18.75 m) long or 9'-6" (2.9 m) wide or 44 tonnes total weight SLOW means 5 mph or less

At automatic level crossings, drivers of large or slow vehicles must phone before and after crossing

DRIVERS OF LONG LOW VEHICLES phone before crossing

Long low vehicles may be at risk of grounding; drivers of such vehicles must phone before crossing

Countdown markers may be provided on the approach to a crossing. These divide the distance between the advance warning sign and the stop line into three equal parts; each sloping bar does not necessarily represent a distance of 100 yards

NEW LEVEL CROSSING CONTROL AHEAD

New method of controlling traffic at a crossing ahead (temporary sign)

At the crossing

Some crossings have flashing red road traffic signals; these mean **STOP** (and this applies to pedestrians too). A steady amber light shows before the red lights begin to flash, as at ordinary road traffic signals; this means **STOP** unless it is unsafe to do so. If the red lights flash for more than three minutes without a train arriving (other than at crossings with full barriers), or any barrier is lowered without the lights flashing, phone the signal operator. When the barriers rise, do not proceed until the signals go out. If your vehicle breaks down or stalls on a crossing, get yourself and your passengers out of the vehicle as soon as possible. Phone the signal operator and follow the instructions given. Stand well clear of the crossing if the alarm sounds, the signals show or the barriers lower.

ANOTHER TRAIN COMING if lights continue to show

Road traffic signals at a level crossing

Direction to phone

Location of phone

Flashing pedestrian signals used at some level crossings indicate that it is not safe to cross: pedestrians should stop at the pedestrian stop line

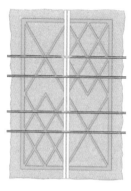

Yellow box markings indicate an area of carriageway at a level crossing that must be kept clear. Do not enter the box if other stationary traffic may cause you to stop with any part of your vehicle within the box

Name of level crossing and phone number for contacting the railway operator (at level crossings without a dedicated phone)

Place where drivers of large or slow vehicles should park near a level crossing while contacting the signal operator

Automatic half-barrier level crossings

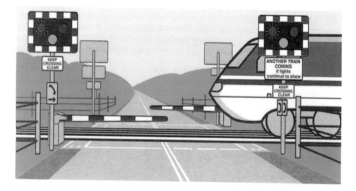

Amber lights and audible warnings followed by flashing red lights warn that a train is approaching and that the barriers are about to come down. You must **STOP**. The red lights flash all the time the barriers are down, but the audible warning might stop. If another train is approaching, the barriers will stay down; the lights will continue to flash and, if there is an audible warning, the sound will change.

Level crossings with miniature warning lights

These level crossings have gates or barriers but no attendant. The miniature red and green lights are operated by an approaching train. Full directions for using these crossings are given on roadside signs. You must stop even if the gates or barriers have been left open. Always close the gates or barriers after crossing.

Open level crossings

The St Andrew's cross is used at level crossings where there are no gates or barriers. At automatic crossings, **you must always STOP when the traffic light signals show**. At crossings with "give way" signs, **always look out for and give way to trains**.

Automatic open level crossings have flashing signals and audible warnings. The lights will flash and the warnings will sound until it is safe to cross

If there is more than one railway line over an automatic crossing, this signal will also flash and the sound of the audible warning will change if another train is approaching

Open level crossings without gates, barriers or road traffic light signals have "give way"signs over a symbol of a railway locomotive

Tram signs, signals and road markings

Trams can run on roads used by other vehicles and pedestrians. The part of the road used by trams (the "swept path") may have a different colour or textured surface to the rest of the road, or it may be edged with special road markings. **Keep the "swept path" clear.** Trams cannot move out of the way of other road users!

Route for trams only (and buses where the upper sign also includes the bus symbol)

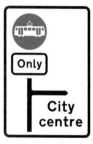

Indication of a tram-only route at a junction ahead

Warning of trams crossing the road ahead

Road marking indicating the start of a route for trams only (and buses when varied to TRAM & BUS ONLY)

Reminder to pedestrians to look out for trams approaching from both directions

Drivers of other vehicles must give way to trams at level crossings without barriers, gates or road traffic light signals. Sometimes just a "give way" sign and a tram plate may be used

30

Examples of signs, signals and road markings for tram drivers

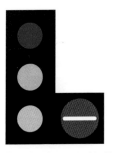

The signal mounted to the right gives instructions to tram drivers; these instructions may not be the same as those given to drivers of other vehicles

Stop unless it is unsafe to do so

Stop

Proceed ahead

Proceed left

Proceed right

Stop line for trams at traffic signals where that part of the road is not used by other vehicles

Speed limit sign for tram drivers shown in kilometres per hour. All diamond-shaped signs are for tram drivers only

31

Bus and cycle signs and road markings

No vehicles designed to carry more than 8 passengers (excluding driver) or local buses

With-flow bus lane ahead that can also be used by pedal cycles and taxis. Hours of operation may be shown

With-flow bus and pedal cycle lane sign showing hours of operation

Route for buses and pedal cycles only (cycles not admitted when cycle symbol not shown; taxis admitted when "taxi" shown in upper sign)

The word "local" on the bus symbol means the only buses that may use the lane are those running a local service. Where the word "local" is not shown, the lane may be used by any vehicle designed to carry more than 8 passengers, excluding the driver, and local buses. Solo motorcycles may use the lane where the motorcycle symbol is shown on the signs (see page 141). Other vehicles may enter and stop in a bus lane to load and unload unless signs alongside the lane indicate otherwise.

Road marking indicating the start of a route for buses only. TAXI and/or the cycle symbol may be included

Bus lane road marking

Traffic may use both lanes at the end of a bus lane

Where there is a break in a bus lane at a junction, other traffic may use the left-hand lane for turning left only

Bus lane on road at junction ahead

End of bus lane

Contra-flow bus lane (the upward arrows indicate the number of traffic lanes available)

Contra-flow bus and pedal cycle lane on road at junction ahead

Road marking for a contra-flow bus lane that is also used by pedal cycles

Reminder to pedestrians to look out for buses or buses and pedal cycles approaching from the right

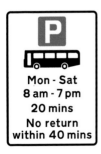

Parking place for buses only, during times shown (with time limit)

Parking place for buses only (no time limit)

Bus Stop

Stopping place
for buses

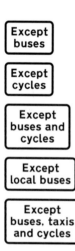

Photostop only
10 am - 4 pm

Stopping place for
tourist buses to
allow passengers to
take photographs

Except
buses

Except
cycles

Except
buses and
cycles

Except
local buses

Except
buses, taxis
and cycles

Plates used to indicate
exemptions for buses,
taxis and pedal cycles
from prohibitions such
as turn left ahead and
no left turn. These signs
may be circular when
mounted in combination
with traffic signals

Place where local
buses may stand,
from which all
other vehicles are
prohibited during
the times shown

Stopping by
vehicles other
than local buses
prohibited during
the times shown

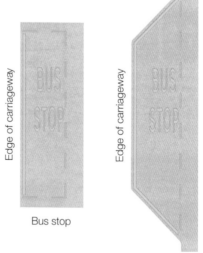

Bus stop

Bus stop
in a lay-by

The broad continuous yellow line at the
edge of the carriageway means that other
vehicles are prohibited from stopping

**BUSES
ONLY**

Entrance to a
bus station,
depot or garage

Mandatory with-flow pedal cycle lane ahead. Hours of operation may be shown

Mandatory with-flow pedal cycle lane. Other vehicles must not use this part of the carriageway except to pick up or set down passengers. Hours of operation may be shown

Route recommended for pedal cycles on the main carriageway of a road. This may be marked as an advisory pedal cycle lane

Mandatory contra-flow pedal cycle lane (the upward arrows indicate the number of traffic lanes available)

Road markings for a mandatory pedal cycle lane

Road markings for an advisory pedal cycle lane. Other vehicles should not use this part of the carriageway unless it is unavoidable

Contra-flow pedal cycles in a one-way street (other than a mandatory contra-flow cycle lane). This may be marked by a broken line on the carriageway or there may be no line at all

Pedal cycle lane on road at junction ahead or (where "lane" is varied to "track") cycle track crossing road at junction ahead

Reminder to pedestrians to look out for pedal cycles approaching from the right

End of cycle lane, track or route

Road marking indicating the end of a cycle lane, track or route

Shared route for pedal cycles and pedestrians only

Separated track and path for pedal cycles and pedestrians

Route for pedal cycles only

Riding of pedal cycles prohibited

Road marking separating cyclists and pedestrians on a shared route (may be a raised line up to 20 mm high)

Parking place for pedal cycles

No through road except for pedal cycles

Advanced stop line for pedal cycles at traffic signals. When the signals are red, drivers of other vehicles must wait behind the first stop line. If the signals change to red when a vehicle is crossing the first line, the driver must stop at the second line. Drivers should allow time and space for cyclists to move off when the signals change to green

Pedal cycle route crossing or joining road ahead

Pedal cyclists to dismount at end of, or break in, a cycle lane, track or route

Plates used with "cycle route ahead" sign

Pedestrian zone signs

Areas such as shopping streets may be signed as "pedestrian zones". Depending on the extent of the vehicle entry restrictions, such areas may be paved without the usual separation between footway and carriageway and may not have yellow lines and kerb markings to indicate waiting and loading restrictions. Instead restrictions are detailed on zone entry signs and repeater plates. The entry signs may indicate that buses, taxis, disabled badge holders or permit holders may enter the zone. Various examples of zone entry signs are shown below.

All vehicles, including ridden pedal cycles, prohibited. (The hours during which a part-time zone operates will be shown in this panel and exemptions in a lower panel)

The yellow panels indicate that there are waiting restrictions within the zone

Signs without yellow panels are used where access may be more restrictive and where waiting restrictions, if any, are indicated by yellow lines within the zone

Ridden pedal cycles permitted within the zone. (The hours during which a part-time zone operates will be shown in this panel and exemptions in a lower panel)

Where different entry restrictions apply at different times of the day, and these restrictions are too complicated to show on the zone entry sign, a sign that can change its display (a variable message sign) may be used. It is therefore important always to check the restrictions in force before entering the zone.

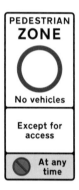 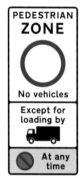

Example of a variable message zone entry sign showing alternative displays for the middle panel (exemptions)

Two examples of waiting restriction repeater signs within the zone. (There may be no yellow lines or kerb markings)

At the end of the zone, a "zone ends" sign will be displayed. The prohibitory roundel in the upper panel will be a grey version of the roundel shown on the entry sign

On-street parking control signs and road markings

Waiting restrictions

Waiting prohibited 24 hours a day, 7 days a week, for at least 4 consecutive months. Yellow plates are no longer used where the restriction applies all year round

Waiting prohibited between times shown on the sign

Waiting restrictions are indicated by both signs and road markings. The restrictions usually apply to the whole of the highway, including verges and footways. Drivers may stop to pick up or set down passengers and, where not prohibited, to load and unload. Disabled blue badge holders can usually park for up to three hours or, in Scotland, without a time limit (see *The Blue Badge Scheme – Explanatory Book* published by the Department for Transport; visit www.dft.gov.uk).

Yellow lines along the edge of the carriageway, parallel to the kerb, indicate that restrictions are in force. In environmentally sensitive areas, a pale shade of yellow may be used and the width of the lines may be reduced. Except in controlled parking zones (see page 52), small yellow plates are normally erected adjacent to the carriageway to give details of the times of operation of the restrictions. Where the yellow plate does not indicate the days of the week, the restrictions apply at the same times every day, including Sunday. If a bank holiday falls on a day when the restrictions are in operation, the restrictions apply in the normal way unless the plate states that they do not. Special restrictions may apply on days when a large event is being held at a nearby stadium or arena; these will also be shown on the plates.

A double yellow line means no waiting at any time. The accompanying yellow plate, "no waiting at any time", is gradually being phased out. Where the "at any time" restriction applies for only part of the year (e.g. during the summer months at a holiday resort) and is for at least four consecutive months, double yellow lines are used with plates giving the dates that the restrictions apply. Waiting restrictions that apply for a shorter period or for only part of the day or week are indicated by a single yellow line.

This "no waiting" sign is used on portable signs to mark temporary waiting restrictions

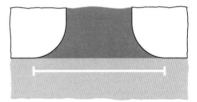

Length of road to be kept clear of stationary vehicles, at entrances to off-street premises or where the kerb is dropped to provide a convenient crossing place for pedestrians

Loading restrictions

Where loading restrictions apply in addition to waiting restrictions ("loading" means both loading and unloading), these are indicated by both yellow kerb marks and white plates. These plates may be combined with the yellow "no waiting" plates. As the marks are placed intermittently along the kerb, a white plate is normally erected at the first mark (where the loading restriction begins) and may include an arrow indicating the direction along the road in which the loading restriction applies. Where a white plate does not indicate the days of the week, the restrictions apply at the same times every day, including Sunday. If a bank holiday falls on a day when the restrictions are in operation, the restrictions apply in the normal way unless the plate states that they do not.

No loading at any time

Loading prohibited 24 hours a day, 7 days a week, for at least 4 consecutive months. The plate should include dates if the restriction does not apply throughout the year

No loading Mon - Fri 8.00 - 9.30 am 4.30 - 6.30 pm

Loading prohibited between times shown on the sign

Special restrictions may apply on days when a large event is being held at a nearby stadium or arena; these will also be shown on the plates. Disabled blue badge holders may not park when loading restrictions are in force.

A double kerb mark means no loading at any time and is always supplemented by a "no loading at any time" plate. Where the "at any time" restriction applies for only part of the year (e.g. during the summer months at a holiday resort) and is for at least four consecutive months, double kerb marks are used with plates giving the dates that the restrictions apply. Loading restrictions that apply for a shorter period or for only part of the day or week are indicated by a single kerb mark.

Examples of waiting and loading restriction signs and markings

At any time 1 May - 30 Sept

No waiting at any time during the summer months in the direction of the arrow. No waiting at any time throughout the year in the opposite direction (no yellow plate required). The changeover point is indicated in the carriageway by the transverse mark on the double yellow lines

41

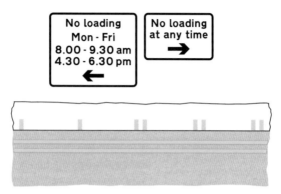

No waiting at any time throughout the year in both directions. No loading to the left during the days and times shown. No loading at any time throughout the year in the opposite direction. The white plates with arrows are placed at the changeover point. There is no transverse mark on the double yellow line because the waiting restrictions do not change

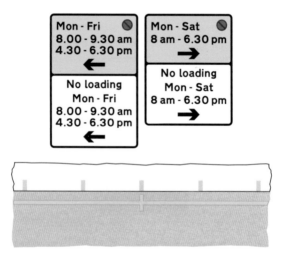

No waiting and loading to the left during morning and evening peak hours on the days shown. No waiting and loading to the right from morning to evening on the days shown. The changeover point for the waiting restrictions is shown by the transverse mark on the single yellow line. The times shown for peak periods and day-time restrictions may vary

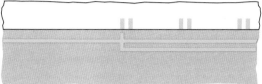

No waiting to the left during the days and times indicated. Loading is permitted at all times in this direction. Waiting and loading prohibited to the right at all times throughout the year

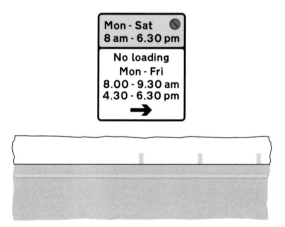

The prohibition of waiting shown on the upper yellow panel on the plate applies in both directions. The prohibition of loading shown on the lower white panel of the plate applies only in the direction of the arrow. In the other direction, loading is permitted at all times. The arrow applies only to the white panel on which it is placed, not to the whole plate. There is no transverse mark on the single yellow line because the waiting restrictions do not change

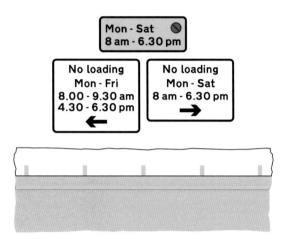

The prohibition of waiting shown on the yellow plate applies in both directions. No loading to the left during morning and evening peak hours on the days shown. No loading to the right from morning to evening on the days shown. The white plates with arrows are placed at the changeover point. There is no transverse mark on the single yellow line because the waiting restrictions do not change. The times shown for peak periods and day-time restrictions may vary

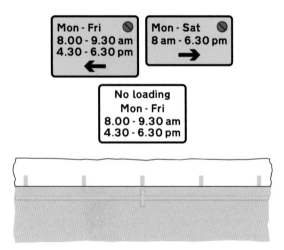

No waiting to the left during morning and evening peak hours. No waiting to the right from morning to evening on the days shown. No loading during morning and evening peak hours in both directions. The changeover point for the waiting restrictions is shown by the transverse mark on the single yellow line

On-street parking places

On-street parking places may be designated for a particular class of vehicle (e.g. solo motorcycles) or for a particular user (e.g. permit holders or disabled badge holders). Parking may be free or paid for (e.g. "pay and display" or parking meters). There may be a time limit on the period of stay and a minimum time before returning to a particular parking place. Some bays may be designated for use by more than one class of vehicle or user, either at the same time or at different times during the day.

Bays are generally marked in white, and are either continuous or divided into individual spaces. They may include words on the carriageway indicating the use of the bay (e.g. DISABLED). Plates are normally erected adjacent to the carriageway to give details of the parking controls. Where a plate does not indicate the days of the week, the restrictions apply at the same times on every day, including Sunday. Where the time of day is not shown, the controls apply for 24 hours. If a bank holiday falls on a day when the controls are in operation, the controls apply in the normal way unless the plate states that they do not. Special controls may apply on days when a large event is being held at a nearby stadium or arena; these will also be shown on the plates.

Edge of carriageway

Parking bay with individual spaces (parallel to the kerb)

Edge of carriageway

Parking bay with individual spaces (echelon)

45

Edge of carriageway

Continuous parking bay adjacent to the kerb (words may be added outside the bay to describe the type of parking)

Continuous parking bay in the centre of the carriageway (the words are omitted where there is no restriction on the type of user)

Solo motorcycles

Motor cars

Car and caravan, or motor caravan

Goods vehicles

The above signs indicate free on-street parking places reserved at all times, with no time limit, for particular classes of vehicles. Other signs may indicate more specific parking controls.

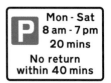

Free parking for all vehicles from Monday to Saturday between 8 am and 7 pm, with a 20-minute time limit (no limit outside those times)

Free parking for motor cars only, from Monday to Saturday between 8 am and 7 pm, with a 20-minute time limit

Free parking for solo motorcycles only, with a one-hour limit at all times

46

Parking for disabled badge holders only, at all times. Older signs may still show the orange badge symbol; these should be replaced by the end of 2009

Parking for permit holders only, at all times

Parking for holders of permit "A2" only, from Monday to Saturday between 8 am and 6 pm

On-street pay and display parking (the arrow points towards the ticket machine). Days of the week and time periods may be added to indicate when parking must be paid for

Location of ticket machine for on-street pay and display parking

Reminder to pay and display at on-street parking place

Pre-paid voucher parking only, from Monday to Saturday between 9 am and 6 pm, with a two-hour time limit (lower panel may give details of voucher)

Where parking-place controls do not operate at all times, any vehicle may park in the bay without payment or time limit unless other restrictions are indicated on the signs.

The upper panel indicates that waiting is prohibited during the morning and evening peak hours (a single yellow line will run through the bay). The lower panel indicates time-limited parking on Monday to Saturday between 10 am and 4 pm. Between 6 pm and 8 am the next day, and all day Sunday, there are no restrictions on parking

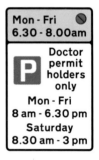

This sign indicates a parking place provided for doctors during the day-time, with a prohibition of waiting between 6.30 am and 8 am (a single yellow line will run through the bay). These restrictions apply from Monday to Friday, with the bay also reserved for doctors on Saturday between 8.30 am and 3 pm

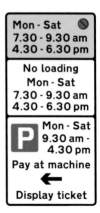

The top panel indicates that waiting is prohibited during the morning and evening peak hours (a single yellow line will run through the bay). The middle panel indicates that loading and unloading are also prohibited during the peak hours (there will be yellow kerb marks alongside the bay). The bottom panel indicates that the bay is used for pay and display parking on Monday to Saturday between 9.30 am and 4.30 pm. Between 6.30 pm and 7.30 am the next day, and all day Sunday, there are no restrictions on parking or loading

Parking bays may be reserved for more than one type of user –
at the same time, at different times, or a combination of both.

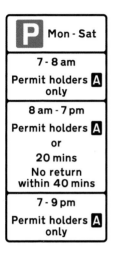

The top panel indicates that the parking
controls apply from Monday to Saturday.
Between 7 am and 8 am, and between 7 pm
and 9 pm, the parking bay may be used only
by permit holders. Between 8 am and 7 pm,
the bay may be used by permit holders with
no time limit, or by any other vehicle with a
20-minute time limit. At all other times and
on Sunday the bay may be used by any
vehicle without any time limit

The parking controls apply from Monday to
Saturday between 7.30 am and 6.30 pm.
During these times the bay may be used by
permit holders, with no time limit, or by any
other vehicle with a 20-minute time limit

The parking bay is reserved for permit
holders, without time limit, at all times.
Other vehicles may also use the bay,
but only from Monday to Saturday between
10 am and 4 pm, with a 20-minute time limit

Although vehicles should not generally be parked on verges and footways (it is unlawful in London and some other cities), this may be allowed on certain narrow streets where parked vehicles would not obstruct pedestrians. There are special signs to indicate footway parking. There may also be white bays indicating where parking is permitted. Where there are controls applying to the parking place, such as pay and display, these should be indicated by separate signs.

Vehicles may be parked partially on the verge or footway

Vehicles may be parked wholly on the verge or footway

Vehicles may be parked partially on the verge or footway during the times shown

End of verge or footway parking

Vehicles may be parked partially on the footway in marked bays only

Some residential streets, particularly culs-de-sac, which are reserved for permit holder parking only may not have any signs or bay markings within them, except possibly for a few repeater plates. A sign at the entrance to the street will indicate that parking is for permit holders only.

Parking for permit holders only in the street or streets beyond this sign, during the times shown

Loading bays and loading areas

Special loading bays may be provided along with parking bays, or in areas where waiting and loading are otherwise prohibited. The bays may be reserved for use by goods vehicles (where indicated on signs) or may be used by all vehicles, e.g. outside shops where heavy purchases have to be carried to a car. However, these bays should not be used prior to making the purchase, but only for collection of pre-paid items when they are too large or heavy to carry to where the car is parked. Once loading is complete, the vehicle must leave the bay. Some loading bays may be used for other purposes at different times of the day. For example, the bay may be reserved for blue badge holders during the day and for loading during early morning and late afternoon. In such cases the bay will **not** be marked "LOADING ONLY"; it is therefore important to read the upright signs to see who can use the bay at certain times of day. There may be times, such as morning and evening peak periods, when loading is not permitted. In such cases there will be a single yellow line running through the bay and single "no loading" marks on the kerb.

Edge of carriageway

Bay reserved
for loading and
unloading by
all vehicles at
all times

Loading bay (conditions of use
shown on upright sign)

Bay reserved for
loading and
unloading by goods
vehicles only during
the times shown

Waiting and loading
are prohibited from
Monday to Saturday
during the times
shown in the top and
middle panels. The
bay may be used for
loading only during
the times shown in
the bottom panel,
including Sunday

51

Off-highway areas may be designated "loading areas" where waiting is restricted except by permitted vehicles. Signs are used without road markings to indicate this.

Entrance to
a loading area

Repeater sign within
a loading area

End of
loading area

Controlled parking zones

Entrance to a
controlled
parking zone

End of controlled
or voucher
parking zone

Some areas are designated as controlled parking zones. The entry sign indicates the times when waiting is prohibited. The yellow lines within the zone **do not normally have yellow plates** indicating the times of the prohibition unless the times are different from those shown on the entry sign. It is therefore important to note the times shown when entering the zone. If there is no lower panel showing days and times, the zone operates at all times. If loading is prohibited at the same time as the waiting prohibition, the entry sign should include the words "No loading" at the bottom of the upper panel. The zone is likely to include parking places and loading bays. Some parking places may be for permit holders only, others for general use. The times when these operate should be shown on the signs at the bays; these times may not be the same as those shown on the zone entry sign. Where the majority of on-street parking within the zone is pay and display, the heading on the entry sign may say "Pay and Display ZONE" instead of "Controlled ZONE".

Other headings might be "Meter ZONE" where there are parking meters, or "Disc ZONE" where a parking disc showing the time of arrival has to be displayed on the vehicle when parking. The entry sign to a pre-paid voucher parking zone includes the voucher logo.

Disc Zone

P Mon - Sat
8 am - 6 pm
30 mins
No return
within 1 hour

Sign at a parking bay within a disc zone. Free parking for all vehicles, with a 30-minute time limit from Monday to Saturday between 8 am and 6 pm. A parking disc indicating the time of arrival at the parking bay must be displayed in the vehicle

Voucher parking **ZONE**

Mon - Sat
9 am - 6 pm
2 hour limit

Entrance to a voucher parking zone

In some areas, local authorities operate special goods vehicle waiting restrictions. Usually these apply to goods vehicles of over 5 or 7.5 tonnes maximum gross weight. Where the same restrictions apply throughout a zone, usually overnight, the times are indicated on a zone entry sign. Within the zone there are no yellow lines (unless there are other waiting restrictions applying to all vehicles), but there should be repeater signs on each side of every street as a reminder. There are equivalent signs for buses with the bus symbol, and signs that apply to both goods vehicles and buses.

5t
ZONE

Mon - Fri
Midnight - 7 am
8 pm - Midnight
Sat & Sun
At any time

Zone entry

5t
Mon - Fri
Midnight - 7 am
8 pm - Midnight
Sat & Sun
At any time

Repeater sign indicating the times when waiting by goods vehicles over the maximum gross weight shown is prohibited

5t
Zone
ENDS

Zone exit

Restricted parking zones

In some environmentally sensitive areas, where waiting and loading restrictions are uniform, they may be indicated by upright repeater signs, but not yellow lines and kerb marks. These are known as restricted parking zones. The zone entry sign indicates the times when waiting and loading are prohibited. Where parking and loading are permitted, usually in signed bays, this should be indicated on the entry signs. The bays within the zone may be fully marked in the conventional manner or indicated by other means such as a change in surface materials. Upright signs will give details about the use of the bays.

Entrance to a restricted parking zone where both waiting and loading are prohibited during the times shown in the lower panel. The words "No loading" are omitted where loading is not prohibited

Entrance to a restricted parking zone where both waiting and loading are prohibited at all times, but where parking and loading bays have been provided. The words "No loading" are omitted where loading is not prohibited

Repeater sign within a restricted parking zone. The lower panel is omitted where loading is not prohibited

End of restricted parking zone

Clearways

The red cross means no stopping, not even to pick up or set down passengers. The sign is used to indicate a 24-hour clearway (usually on a rural road) or may be incorporated into other signs with the words "No stopping" (e.g. the "no stopping except local buses" sign at bus stops). On a 24-hour clearway, the prohibition of stopping applies only to the main carriageway. You may stop in a lay-by unless there are signs to say otherwise. A 24-hour clearway does not have any special road markings, but there should be smaller repeater signs at approximately one mile intervals.

Start of 24-hour clearway (no stopping on main carriageway at any time for the distance shown)

End of 24-hour clearway

This sign is used on a 24-hour clearway where waiting is prohibited on the verge or footway in addition to the prohibition of stopping on the main carriageway. The words "on verge or footway" may be varied to "on verge" or "on footway". Where the "no waiting" symbol is replaced by the red cross, stopping on the verge or footway is prohibited

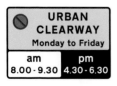

In built-up areas, urban clearways may be provided. During the times the urban clearway is in operation, stopping is not allowed on the carriageway or verges, except to pick up or set down passengers. There are no special road markings, but the signs are repeated throughout the length of the clearway

URBAN
CLEARWAY
End

End of urban clearway

Stopping in lay-by not allowed, except in an emergency (similar to hard shoulders on a motorway). This may not apply to the whole lay-by. The length over which stopping is prohibited will be indicated by double yellow lines. These lay-bys usually have an emergency telephone

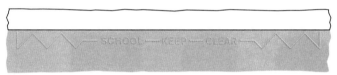

Yellow zig-zag markings outside schools, hospitals or fire, police or ambulance stations indicate the length of road where you should not stop, not even to pick up or set down children or other passengers. Where there is an upright sign, there is a mandatory prohibition of stopping during the times shown. These markings are provided outside schools to ensure that children can see and be seen clearly when crossing the road

Red routes

On red routes, yellow waiting restriction lines are replaced by red lines that mean no stopping for any purpose, not even to pick up or set down passengers, other than by a licensed taxi. A driver of a vehicle displaying a blue badge may stop to pick up or set down a disabled person, but must not park.

Double red lines mean
no stopping at any time

Single red lines mean no stopping during the days and times shown on the upright sign

The prohibition of stopping applies to the whole road, including the verge and footway, during the times shown on upright signs that face oncoming traffic. Special bays marked on the carriageway may be provided for parking or loading; the conditions that apply to these will be indicated on upright signs that should also face oncoming traffic.

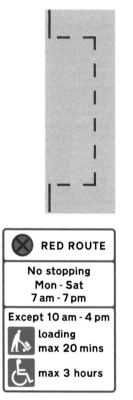

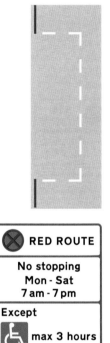

A bay marked with red broken lines means that it is available for use for only part of the time that the red route "no stopping" rule applies. The bay must not be used from Monday to Saturday between 7 am and 10 am nor between 4 pm and 7 pm. In this example, the bay may be used for loading/unloading (max stay 20 minutes) and by blue badge holders (max stay 3 hours), during the times shown in the bottom panel

A bay marked with white broken lines means that it is available for use at all times that the red route "no stopping" rule applies. The upright sign shown in this example means that the bay is reserved for blue badge holders, with a maximum stay of 3 hours

Licensed taxis may pick up or set down passengers at bus stops on a red route where there is a broad continuous yellow line at the edge of the carriageway, but not if the broad line is red. Drivers of vehicles displaying a blue disabled badge are not permitted to stop for any purpose in a bus stop bay where there is either a broad yellow or broad red line

Some red routes have upright signs without any road markings. These are designated "RED ROUTE CLEARWAYS", where stopping for any purpose is prohibited at all times, except in marked lay-bys. Unlike the 24-hour clearway on rural roads, stopping on a red route clearway is prohibited on the verge and footway as well as on the main carriageway. There should be red lines at junctions to warn drivers entering the clearway from a side road.

Start of a red route clearway
(also used as a repeater sign,
particularly after a road junction)

End of red route
clearway

Taxi ranks

Taxi ranks usually have yellow bays marked with the word "TAXIS". Where the bay is used for other purposes (e.g. loading and unloading) at a different time of day, the bay will be white without any words. Either waiting or stopping will be prohibited within a taxi rank. Where stopping is prohibited, the bay includes a broad continuous yellow line at the edge of the carriageway. Where waiting is prohibited in taxi ranks, yellow "no waiting" lines are provided where waiting is also prohibited at other times, or where the bay marking is white because it has shared use. Yellow upright signs show the times when waiting or stopping is prohibited in the rank.

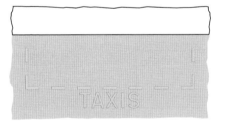

No waiting in taxi rank during the times shown

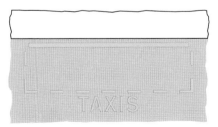

No stopping in taxi rank during the times shown. The bay includes a broad continuous line to indicate the prohibition of stopping

Waiting is prohibited at all times (indicated by double yellow lines). The taxi rank operates from 11 pm to 5 am every day

The taxi rank operates every day between 10 am and 4 pm. Waiting is otherwise prohibited from 8 am to 6 pm every day, and loading is prohibited during the morning and evening peak hours from Monday to Friday

The sign shows the times when the bay is used as a taxi rank (overnight) and when it is used for loading by goods vehicles (during the day from Monday to Saturday). At other times there are no restrictions on parking. The single yellow line is replaced by a broad yellow line if stopping by other vehicles is prohibited during the times the bay is used by taxis. This will be indicated in the upper panel of the sign, where the "no waiting" symbol is replaced by the red cross and the words "No waiting" varied to "No stopping"

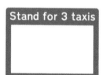

Information boards may be provided at taxi ranks

Road markings

Along the road

Centre line on a single carriageway road

Lane line separating traffic travelling in the same direction (single or dual carriageway road)

Hazard warning line (replaces a centre line or a lane line). An upright sign may indicate the nature of the hazard, such as a bend. The marking is used also on the approach to a junction

Diagonal white lines (hatched markings) bounded by broken lines may be used in the centre of the road to separate opposing flows of traffic. They are often provided at junctions to protect traffic turning right. They may also be used on the approach to a central traffic island or the start of a dual carriageway. Hatched markings with a single, broken boundary line may be used at the edge of the road or next to the central reservation of a dual carriageway: the diagonal lines always slope towards the direction of travel. You should not enter any hatched area bounded by a broken line unless it is safe to do so

Part of the carriageway where traffic passes in the same direction on either side of the chevron marking. Vehicles should not enter the area unless safe to do so. This marking is likely to be found in one-way streets with central islands and where an exit lane leaves at a junction

Part of the carriageway where traffic passes in the same direction on either side of the chevron marking. The continuous boundary line means that vehicles must not enter the area except in an emergency. This marking is used where slip roads leave and join motorways and many dual carriageway roads. It is also used for segregated left-turn lanes at roundabouts

Reduction in the number of lanes, or area not available to traffic. Vehicles must not cross the continuous white line except in an emergency. Used on the right-hand side of a motorway, dual carriageway road or slip road

Arrow indicating the direction in which to pass hatched markings and double white lines, or the route that high vehicles should take under a low arch bridge (may be reversed)

Double white lines

These are used to prevent overtaking where visibility is restricted, and to separate opposing traffic flows on steep hills with climbing lanes. Double continuous lines are also sometimes used on other single carriageway roads that have two lanes in at least one direction. Viewed in the direction of travel, if the line closest to you is continuous, you **must not** cross or straddle it (except to turn into or out of a side road or property, avoid a stationary vehicle blocking the lane, or overtake a pedal cycle, horse or road works vehicle moving at not more than 10 mph). Where the line closest to you is broken, you may cross the lines to overtake if it is safe to do so. Stopping is prohibited on any length of road that has double white lines, even if the line on that side of the road is broken. The exceptions are stopping to pick up or set down passengers, or to load or unload. In these circumstances, you should park off the main carriageway wherever possible.

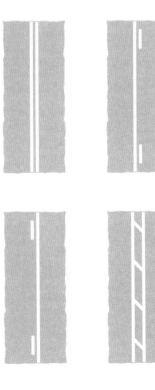

Some double continuous white lines have narrow areas of hatched lines within them or a wider area of hatching to the side. You must not cross a continuous white line to enter a hatched area

Along the edge of the road

Edge of carriageway, other than at junctions, exits from private drives and lay-bys. Used on the left-hand side of the road and alongside the central reservation of dual carriageway roads

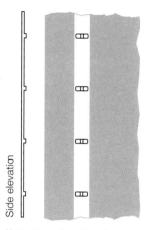

Side elevation

Alternative edge of carriageway marking, with raised ribs to provide audible and tactile warnings when the line is being crossed. They are used on motorways and other roads with hard shoulders or hard marginal strips

Edge of main carriageway at a junction (particularly where a slip road leaves or joins), at an exit from a private drive or at a lay-by. Also used to divide the main carriageway from a traffic lane that leaves the main carriageway at a junction ahead (lane drop)

Edge of main carriageway at a junction or at an exit from a private drive. Used in conjunction with "give way" markings on the side road

65

At junctions

Do not cross chevron markings with a continuous boundary line

See "Regulatory signs" for "give way" (and "stop") priority junctions

Diverge arrow indicating an exit slip road or the start of a lane for turning traffic (may be reversed)

Hatched area to protect turning traffic. Drivers should not enter unless it is safe to do so

Road junction with a right-turn lane

Motorway or dual carriageway road with exit and entry slip roads

66

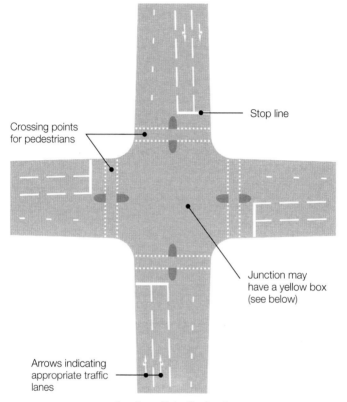

Stop line

Crossing points for pedestrians

Junction may have a yellow box (see below)

Arrows indicating appropriate traffic lanes

Junction with traffic signals

Where stationary traffic would be likely to block a junction, a yellow box may be marked on the road, covering all or part of the junction. You must not enter the box if your exit is not clear. If turning right at the junction, you may enter the box (behind other right-turning vehicles, if any) to wait for a gap in the oncoming traffic, but only if the right-turn exit is clear

Some roundabouts may have lane markings to guide drivers to the appropriate exit and are often controlled by traffic signals

Single broken "give way" line

Some roundabouts have yellow bar markings on the approach. These become closer together the nearer to the roundabout and provide a warning to drivers to slow down

Conventional roundabout

A mini-roundabout is normally found on a road with a speed limit of 30 mph or less. It should be treated the same as a conventional roundabout. You must give way to traffic from the right, and keep to the left of the white circle unless the size of your vehicle or the junction layout makes driving over it unavoidable

Mini-roundabout

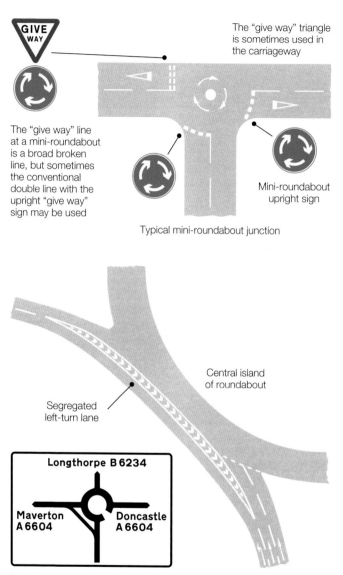

The "give way" triangle is sometimes used in the carriageway

The "give way" line at a mini-roundabout is a broad broken line, but sometimes the conventional double line with the upright "give way" sign may be used

Mini-roundabout upright sign

Typical mini-roundabout junction

Central island of roundabout

Segregated left-turn lane

Longthorpe B 6234

Maverton A 6604

Doncastle A 6604

Some conventional roundabouts may have a segregated left-turn lane where drivers do not give way to traffic on the roundabout. This may be separated from the roundabout by either a solid island or chevron markings Where the chevrons are bounded by continuous lines, vehicles must not enter the area except in an emergency. You should therefore choose the correct lane well before the roundabout. A directional sign in advance of the junction may show the segregated lane

Traffic lanes at junctions

Appropriate traffic lanes for different movements at junction ahead.
A double-headed arrow is used where two different movements may be
made from the same lane or where that lane divides into two or more
lanes ahead (e.g. a lane with a combined "left" and "ahead" arrow may
divide into a left-turn lane and an ahead lane)

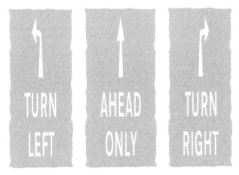

Compulsory traffic movements at a junction ahead.
These may apply to a specific traffic lane or to all
traffic approaching the junction

Direction to be
taken by traffic
turning within a
junction

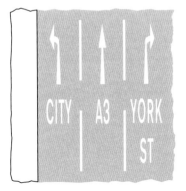

Appropriate traffic lanes
for particular destinations

Worded markings

Direction in which pedestrians should look before crossing the road (particularly in a one-way street or where there is a bus lane)

Area of carriageway to be kept clear of stationary traffic, usually to allow the passage of vehicles into or out of a side road or access. The white bars may be omitted

Vehicles must not pass this marking. May be used with the upright "no entry" sign

Associated with a hazard. There will normally be an upright warning sign

Reflecting road studs

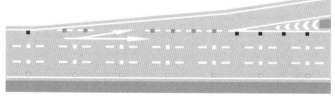

Central reservation

Coloured road studs help drivers at night, especially on wet roads, or in poor visibility. White studs mark traffic lanes or the centre of the road. The left-hand side of the carriageway is marked by red studs, and the edge of the central reservation of a motorway or dual carriageway road by amber studs. Green studs are used to mark lay-bys and the entrances to, and exits from, slip roads.

Traffic calming

Traffic calming is the term used to describe physical features provided along a road to encourage drivers to reduce speed. These features are introduced for the safety of all road users, particularly pedestrians and cyclists. Traffic calming schemes can employ a variety of measures, including road humps and narrowings. Warning signs often indicate the type of measure to be expected. There may be an entry sign at the boundary of an area that has traffic calming features.

Entrance to a traffic-calmed area. The name of the area may be shown. The sign may also be used in advance of the area and show a distance. Where the traffic-calmed area is reached by turning into a side road, the sign will include an arrow

Road humps

Road humps may have a flat or round top, extending across the width of the road or covering a whole junction. They may also be in the form of a "cushion", covering only part of a traffic lane and designed to allow buses and large emergency vehicles to straddle them, whilst slowing other vehicles. Except in a 20 mph zone, warning signs are erected at the beginning of the road where a hump or series of humps is installed.

Road humps for distance shown. May be varied to "Hump" with distance omitted

Alternative plates used with "road hump" sign

Road humps for distance shown and in direction indicated

Road hump for distance shown and in direction indicated

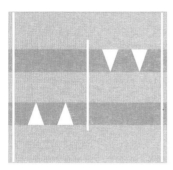

A road hump is normally marked with white triangle and edge line markings.

Zebra and signal-controlled pedestrian crossings are sometimes located on flat-top humps. These may be indicated by advance warning signs.

Humped crossing

Zebra crossing on a road hump

Humped crossing

Signal-controlled pedestrian crossing on a road hump

Road narrowings

Roads may be reduced in width by the use of build-outs on one or both sides. When placed on both sides, they may be opposite each other or staggered. Priority through the narrowing may be controlled by signs and "give way" markings. It is essential that you obey signs indicating priority to vehicles coming from the opposite direction.

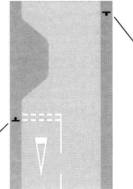

Priority over oncoming vehicles

Give way to oncoming vehicles

If priority is not given to either direction at a road narrowing, you should ensure that you can pass through without endangering occupants in vehicles approaching from the other direction. Do not accelerate on the approach to a narrowing, but maintain a slow steady speed and be prepared to give way to approaching traffic. Let any cyclists proceed ahead of you.

Road narrows on left (right if symbol reversed)

Road narrows on both sides

Warning signs indicating which side the narrowing occurs may be used in advance, especially where priority signs and markings are not provided.

20 mph zones

Entrance to a 20 mph zone

End of 20 mph zone and start of 30 mph speed limit

Some traffic-calmed areas are indicated by the 20 mph zone entry sign. This sign, as well as indicating a 20 mph speed limit, warns drivers that they are entering an area with traffic calming features, such as road humps and road narrowings. These features may not be individually signed, nor are there likely to be 20 mph speed limit repeater signs. In these areas, it is important that you adopt a steady low speed and avoid repeated acceleration and deceleration.

Home Zones

Entrance to a Home Zone

Home Zones are residential areas with streets designed to be places for people as well as for motor traffic. The road space is shared among drivers and other road users. People could be using the whole of the space for a range of activities. You should drive slowly and carefully and be prepared to stop to allow people extra time to make room for you to pass them in safety.

End of Home Zone

Quiet Lanes

Some minor rural roads may be designated as Quiet Lanes. These are appropriate for shared use by walkers, cyclists, horse riders and motor vehicles. You should drive slowly and carefully and be prepared to stop to allow people extra time to make room for you to pass them in safety.

Start of designated Quiet Lane

End of Quiet Lane

Other features

Rumble devices across the road, either in the form of strips or larger areas, may be used to provide a visual, audible and vibratory effect, often in rural locations. The intention is to alert drivers to a hazard ahead, usually a bend or road junction, and encourage them to reduce speed. A warning sign may be used in association with a rumble device to identify the hazard, but the device itself is not the hazard and is not usually specifically signed.

Gateways into villages may be formed from the combination of speed limit signs, yellow backing boards and village name plates. Central hatched markings or islands may also be used to separate opposing traffic. Drivers approaching the gateways should reduce speed and observe the speed limit all the way through the village.

Example of a village gateway

Some parts of the carriageway may have a coloured surface to emphasise the road markings.

Motorway signs, signals and road markings

Most motorway signs have a blue background with white lettering, numbers and borders, although tourist destination signs, as on other roads, have brown backgrounds (see page 84).

Start of motorway regulations

Special traffic regulations govern the use of motorways. These include no stopping (except, in an emergency, on the hard shoulder or verge), no U-turns and no reversing. Goods vehicles and buses (where a bus is a vehicle constructed to carry more than eight seated passengers) with a maximum laden weight of more than 7.5 tonnes, vehicles drawing trailers, and vehicles required to be fitted with a speed limiter, must not use the right-hand lane of a motorway that has three or more lanes. Motorways must not be used by certain classes of traffic: learner drivers other than HGV, invalid carriages of less than 254 kg unladen weight, pedal cycles, motorcycles under 50 cc capacity, agricultural vehicles and vehicles incapable of attaining a speed of 25 mph on the level when unladen and not drawing a trailer. Pedestrians and animals are also prohibited.

To ensure that direction signs are absolutely clear to drivers travelling at motorway speeds, it is necessary to limit the number of destinations shown. Your destination might not appear on the motorway signs: when planning a journey, it is advisable before setting off to check the junction number of the exit you require. Junctions can be identified by the number shown on a black background in the bottom left-hand or top left-hand corner of motorway signs (or, in the case of overhead signs, in a separate panel also indicating the distance to the junction). Junction numbers are usually shown on road maps, so it is easy to check these before starting your journey. On the motorway, these numbers can be used as a guide to your location. However, not all junctions have an exit in both directions, so numbers may not be consecutive. Where new junctions have been constructed, the number may be followed by a letter (e.g. junction 23A).

A road other than a motorway is called an "all-purpose road". At the point where you join a motorway, a special symbol is used to indicate the start of motorway regulations. A direction sign on an all-purpose road will normally use this symbol to indicate a motorway slip road or the beginning of a motorway. Where a sign shows a motorway route number on a blue background without the symbol, the route indicated will normally be an all-purpose road that you should follow to reach the motorway.

Blue direction signs, with the motorway symbol and large route numbers, indicate that a motorway or motorway slip road leads directly from a junction with an all-purpose road. The motorway junction number, shown on the black background, may not always be included

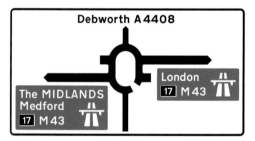

On the approach to a junction with a motorway, a direction sign on an all-purpose road has blue panels that include the motorway symbol. The panels may include the junction number on a black background. The name in capital letters is a regional destination

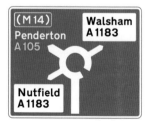

This sign, with the motorway number in brackets on a blue background, but without the motorway symbol, indicates the route to take from a junction ahead in order to reach the motorway. The motorway is not accessed directly from this junction

Signs for junctions on the motorway

On the approach to a junction, direction signs are usually located 1 mile and ½ mile in advance, and at the exit point. Where junctions are close together, these distances may be reduced, normally to ⅔ mile and ⅓ mile respectively. The signs may be mounted at the side of the road or overhead.

Signs located at the side of the motorway. These are used where there is a deceleration lane. The number of lanes through the junction remains the same

The first two signs on the approach to a junction show the destination and the route number for the exit only. The distance shown (usually 1 mile or ½ mile) is the distance to the exit (start of the deceleration lane). The junction number is shown on the black background

This sign is located at the start of the deceleration lane and includes destinations reached by staying on the motorway

A final route direction sign is usually located where the exit slip road separates from the main carriageway

Countdown markers indicate the distance to the start of the deceleration lane. Each bar represents about 100 yards

Overhead sign for junctions with deceleration lanes, where the number of lanes through the junction remains the same

This sign is used on the approach to the junction (usually 1 mile and ½ mile in advance) and at the start of the deceleration lane. Destinations and route numbers are shown for both the exit and the motorway ahead. Countdown markers are normally provided for the deceleration lane

Signs located at the side of the motorway where one or more lanes leave the main carriageway to become the exit slip road. This type of junction is known as a lane drop

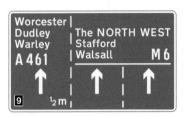

This sign is normally located 1 mile and ½ mile before the junction and shows the appropriate lanes to use for various destinations. In this example, the left-hand lane leads directly to the exit slip road; the centre and right-hand lanes continue through the junction

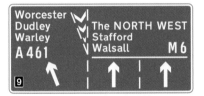

This sign, with the inclined arrow, is normally located just before the left-hand lane leaves the main carriageway

Overhead signs for a lane-drop junction

This sign is used both in advance and at the junction

A confirmatory sign may be provided just after the point where the slip road has separated from the main carriageway. It is used where signs on the approach to the junction are either overhead or located at the side of the motorway

Lane-drop junctions do not use the countdown markers shown on page 79, as there is no deceleration lane for drivers to move into. A special road marking is used at lane drops (see pages 65 and 81) between the main carriageway and the lane that leads to the exit slip road. This marking usually commences at the ½ mile advance sign.

Some junction layouts may be more complex and designed to allow a heavier flow of traffic to leave the motorway. A traffic lane may be shared by traffic both continuing ahead and leaving the motorway. This shared lane has a deceleration lane separated from a lane drop by chevron road markings. In the example, the left-hand lane is used for the exit slip road only, the centre lane is the shared lane, and the right-hand lane is for ahead traffic only. A sign mounted at the side of the motorway shows the road layout. An overhead sign shows the appropriate lanes to use for each destination.

Central reservation

A sign mounted at the side of the motorway shows the arrangement of traffic lanes

Overhead sign showing appropriate lanes for the different destinations

Other types of sign in advance of junctions

Where the junction ahead is with another motorway, additional signs may be provided prior to the 1 mile advance sign

Where two junctions are very close, they may both be shown on the same sign, together with the distances and junction numbers. The sign that is located where the deceleration lane starts for the first exit (see page 79) will normally show the second exit place names and route number with the ahead destinations

This overhead sign indicates a junction that has two exits. The first exit has a deceleration lane and is indicated by the upper part of the sign. The second exit is a lane drop. Traffic continuing along the motorway should use the centre and right-hand lanes

Signs showing lanes that join the main carriageway at junctions

Sign for drivers on slip road

Sign for drivers on main carriageway

The slip road joins the main carriageway as a lane gain to increase the number of lanes from two to three. A distance panel may be added

Sign for drivers on slip road

Sign for drivers on main carriageway

The right-hand lane of the slip road joins the main carriageway as a merge with an acceleration lane. This is followed by the left-hand lane which joins the main carriageway as a lane gain. Chevron road markings normally separate the two lanes on the slip road. The distance may be omitted

Direction signs on exit slip roads (the green panels indicate a primary route; the white panels indicate a non-primary route)

Directions from junction ahead, usually controlled by traffic signals or a "give way" sign

Directions from a roundabout ahead

Motorway-to-motorway junction with a roundabout (motorway regulations continue to apply)

Appropriate lanes to use on the approach to the junction (sign located at the side of the slip road)

Appropriate lanes to use on the approach to the junction (overhead sign over the slip road)

Appropriate lanes for turning movements at junction ahead

Direction signs where the main carriageway of a motorway ends at a roundabout

Motorway ends at a junction with an all-purpose road

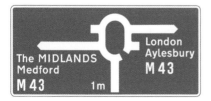

Motorway ends at a junction with another motorway

83

Signs for tourist destinations

Tourist destinations are shown on signs with brown backgrounds. On the main carriageway of a motorway, these are separate from the main direction signs and are usually sited ¾ mile and ¼ mile from the junction (although they do not show the distance to the junction). On exit slip roads and where the motorway ends at a roundabout, the main direction signs may show tourist destinations on a brown panel, in the same way that they show other destinations on green and white panels (see page 83). However, separate brown signs are likely to be used at these locations to avoid putting too much information on a single sign. See pages 100 to 102 for more information about tourist signs.

Sign at the side of the main carriageway. There will usually be two of these in advance of the junction

Sign indicating a place with several tourist attractions. It is located at the side of the main carriageway on the approach to a junction

Sign on exit slip road indicating directions to tourist attractions from a roundabout ahead

Sign on exit slip road indicating directions to tourist attractions from a junction ahead

Where it is not practicable to provide tourist destination signs within 1 mile of a junction or there are more destinations than can be accommodated on the signs, this sign may be used in advance of the main 1 mile direction sign for the junction. It may also be used when the junction layout is complex (such as that shown on page 81); "leave at Junction 24" is then varied to "follow" plus a destination

Signs for motorway service areas

On most motorways, service areas are provided at intervals of not more than 30 miles, half an hour at normal motorway driving speeds. These service areas are open 24 hours a day, every day of the year, and provide fuel, free parking (up to 2 hours), refreshments, toilets and disabled access. Other facilities, including telephones, motels and tourist information, may also be provided. Some motorway service areas are accessed directly from the main carriageway, others via junctions with other roads, where they will also be available to non-motorway traffic.

Services
10 m

After each junction, a sign may show the distance to the next motorway service area

This sign may be used when there is a junction with another motorway before the next service area

About 1 mile in advance of a service area, a sign may inform drivers of the availability of services ahead, including the names of the operators. It will normally show the next two services, and include services on other motorways if the junctions with those motorways are reached before the second service area. Where the first services are located at a junction, this sign is likely to be used about 2 miles in advance; the word "Services" may be added to the junction direction signs as an exit destination

About ½ mile before the service area (further if the services are at a junction), a sign informs drivers of the facilities available, and may include both the name of the operator and the geographical name. The price of fuel, if shown, is usually for a litre of unleaded petrol, indicated by the green pump symbol. The "LPG" symbol means that LPG fuel is available; the "i" symbol refers to an information point; the bed symbol indicates overnight accommodation

Sign located at start of the deceleration lane for a service area with direct access from the motorway

Alternative signs indicating the entrance to a service area accessed directly from a motorway. May be used to indicate the direction to a motorway service area located on an all-purpose road

Where a motorway service area is situated on an all-purpose road, the signs off the motorway, indicating the services, should have a blue background (older signs may have a green or white background). The geographical name of the services may be shown on these signs, but not the operator's name (this is shown only on the signs on the motorway). The word "Services" may be incorporated into other direction signs, including the sign on the exit slip road from the motorway. Where these signs have a green or white background, the word "Services" (with or without a geographical name) will normally be placed on a blue panel.

Motorway service area ahead on an all-purpose road (sign located off the motorway)

Direction or entrance to a motorway service area located on an all-purpose road (alternative signs)

Signs may be provided to indicate that services are not available on the motorway.

Sign on motorway indicating that no services are available ahead. Drivers should leave the motorway if service facilities are required

Sign on all-purpose road indicating that no services are available on motorway ahead. The motorway number may include a compass point (e.g. "M41(N)") if services are available in one direction but not the other

Other signs on motorways

A route confirmatory sign is provided after most junctions. This shows the motorway number and the distances to the main destinations ahead

Where there are more destinations than can be accommodated on the direction signs at a junction, a sign such as this may be used in advance of the 1 mile direction sign. It advises drivers of the route to be followed (or junction to leave at) for destinations that cannot be accommodated on the main junction sign

This sign indicates a slip road that leads to a maintenance compound and is not available to the general public

Where a motorway has been widened but the original bridges retained, there may be no hard shoulder under or over the bridge. Where this occurs, signs will indicate the distance over which this applies. There will be hatched markings on the hard shoulder at the point where it comes to an end

Observation platforms are sometimes provided at the back of the hard shoulder. These are reserved for authorised vehicles, such as those of the Highways Agency's Traffic Officers or the police

HERTFORDSHIRE

County boundary sign (may be varied to show the name of a river)

Marker posts, located at the back of the hard shoulder at 100 metre intervals, show the direction to the nearest emergency telephone (housed in an orange box). You can use the telephone to contact the control centre in case of an emergency or breakdown

Some motorways may have special chevron markings in the centre of the traffic lanes. These are spaced 40 metres apart, and keeping two marks between your vehicle and the one in front will provide a safe driving distance at 70 mph. There will be signs advising you to check your distance, keep two chevrons apart and keep your distance.

Central reservation

Check your distance

Direction signs for drivers of goods vehicles

Direction of route recommended for goods vehicles

This sign is located before the 1 mile advance sign for a junction ahead. It is used where it is not practicable to sign a goods vehicle route at the junction itself

Signs indicating the end of motorway regulations

Sign located at the entrance to a service area accessed directly from the motorway, or a maintenance compound

Sign located on main carriageway to indicate the distance to the end of the motorway

Sign located where the motorway ends on either the main carriageway or exit slip road

Motorway signals and variable signs

These advise of abnormal traffic conditions ahead (e.g. lane closures or fog) and may indicate a speed limit. See Active Traffic Management on page 91 for signs where the hard shoulder is sometimes used as a traffic lane. Where variable speed limit signs are mounted over individual lanes and the speed limit is shown in a red ring (see page 20), the limit is mandatory. Speed limits that do not include the red ring are the maximum speeds advised for the prevailing conditions.

Signals and variable signs may apply to individual lanes when mounted overhead or, when located on the central reservation or at the side of the motorway, to the whole carriageway. They are normally blank, but when they indicate a restriction the reason may not always be obvious. There may have been an accident ahead, so take no chances and obey the signals. When red lamps are flashing above your lane, you **MUST STOP** unless you can move safely to a lane where red signals are not showing.

Red lamps flashing from side to side in pairs, together with a red cross, mean "do not proceed in the traffic lane directly below". These signals are mounted above the carriageway: there is a signal for each traffic lane. A previous signal may direct you into an adjacent lane (see page 90). More than one lane may be closed to traffic

Signals and variable signs above each lane of the motorway

Each lane has its own signal; each signal has two pairs of amber lamps that flash from top to bottom. You should obey the signal for your lane

Temporary maximum speed advised for prevailing traffic conditions

Move to adjacent lane (arrow may point downwards to the right)

Leave motorway at next exit

Risk of fog ahead

Risk of ice ahead

End of temporary restrictions

Signals and variable signs at the side of the motorway

These apply to the carriageway as a whole and are either located on the central reservation or mounted above the hard shoulder in combination with variable signs that display information about road works, congestion and diversions ahead. The amber lamps flash in pairs from top to bottom

Various lane closures (signs for carriageways with four, three or two lanes)

Temporary maximum speed advised

Leave motorway at next exit

Risk of fog ahead

Risk of ice ahead

End of temporary restrictions

Signals and variable signs at the entrance to a motorway

All lanes closed (signs for carriageways with four, three or two lanes). Do not enter the motorway when the red lamps are flashing in pairs from side to side

Older type of motorway signal

On some motorways, particularly in Scotland, you may encounter this type of signal mounted at the side of the carriageway. Flashing amber lamps indicate that there is a hazard ahead. You should not exceed a speed of 30 mph until you have passed this hazard

Active Traffic Management

Start of Active Traffic Management

A scheme has been introduced on part of the M42 motorway, between the M6 and M40 near Birmingham, to allow traffic to use the hard shoulder as a traffic lane during times of heavy congestion or when there has been an incident that blocks one or more lanes. This is known as "Active Traffic Management".

Sign indicating presence of emergency refuge areas ahead

Emergency refuge area SOS

This sign is located at each emergency refuge area

Lay-bys, with emergency telephones, have been constructed at the back of the hard shoulder. These are known as "emergency refuge areas" and should be used in the same way as a normal hard shoulder. Even if the hard shoulder is not being used as a traffic lane, in the event of a breakdown or emergency you should use the refuge areas whenever possible. They are provided at intervals of approximately 500 metres (550 yards). Emergency refuge areas may be provided elsewhere on the motorway network at locations where there are no hard shoulders.

Each lane, including the hard shoulder, has overhead signals and signs similar to those described on pages 89 and 90. Before the hard shoulder is made available to traffic, a speed limit will be applied to the main carriageway. This will be the same for all lanes and will usually be 50 mph. The speed limit shown over each lane will be in a red ring (see page 20) with no signals. There will be a red cross, with no signals, above the hard shoulder to indicate that it is closed. When the hard shoulder is in use as a traffic lane, the red cross will change to a speed limit (the same as for the other lanes). Should it be necessary to close any lane, including the hard shoulder when it is in use as a traffic lane, a red cross with red lamps flashing in vertical pairs will be shown above that lane (see page 89). The previous signal will show an arrow, inclined downwards to the left or to the right, indicating that you should move into the adjacent lane (see page 90).

A variable message sign, located above the hard shoulder, will give worded messages such as "Congestion Stay in lane" and "Congestion Use hard shoulder".

At intermediate junctions, the hard shoulder becomes the exit lane leading directly to the slip road. A sign indicates where this change of use takes place. If the hard shoulder is not already in use as a traffic lane, you can move across to leave the motorway when you have passed the sign. When the hard shoulder is in use as a traffic lane, it should normally be used only by traffic leaving at the next junction, as it becomes a lane drop at the junction (i.e. the lane becomes the exit slip road). The overhead direction signs are slightly different from those on other motorways. Signs in advance of the junction showing the exit destinations and those showing the ahead destinations are usually mounted overhead at separate locations.

↖ A404 High Wycombe

Destination reached by leaving the motorway at the next junction

The NORTH WEST, Birmingham, Coventry (N) M6 ↑

Destinations reached by staying on the motorway at the next junction

The end of Active Traffic Management is indicated by a sign, and the overhead variable signs indicate the resumption of the national speed limit (see page 20).

Visit www.highways.gov.uk/atm for further information on Active Traffic Management.

Direction signs on all-purpose roads

Junction ahead between two primary routes

Roads other than motorways are referred to as all-purpose roads. Those of national and regional importance are called **primary routes**: they always have "A" numbers. Direction signs on these roads have **green backgrounds**, yellow route numbers and white lettering. Primary routes, together with motorways, form a national network of roads between major towns (primary destinations).

Junction ahead between two non-primary routes

All other roads, including local roads with "A" numbers, are called **non-primary routes**. Direction signs on these roads have **white backgrounds**, with black route numbers and lettering. Most road maps show primary routes in green and use other colours to distinguish between non-primary "A" roads, "B" roads and local un-numbered roads. Maps may also indicate primary destinations. The colour coding of these maps and the colours of the traffic signs may help you to plan your journey, using primary routes wherever possible.

Where a primary route has a junction with a non-primary route, a coloured panel on the advance direction sign is used to indicate a route of different status. Blue panels are used to indicate motorways (see page 78), green panels indicate primary routes and white non-primary routes.

Sign on a primary route indicating a non-primary route

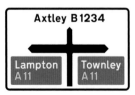

Sign on a non-primary route indicating a primary route

There are different types of sign that might be used on the approach to a junction. A "map-type" sign shows the junction layout and is commonly used for roundabouts, with a special symbol for mini-roundabouts. The width of each route symbol depends on the type of the road indicated: wide for primary routes and motorways, medium for "A" and "B" numbered non-primary routes and narrow for local roads without numbers.

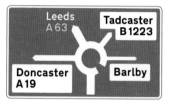

Map-type sign on primary route indicating a roundabout ahead

Map-type sign for a mini-roundabout

A stack-type sign shows directions at a junction ahead, but not the road layout. It can often be smaller than the equivalent map-type sign and is used for simple junctions (e.g. a crossroads) and where there might not be space for a larger sign, especially in urban areas.

Examples of stack-type signs. Arrows indicate the direction of exits from the junction ahead; each is shown on a separate part of the sign. The ahead direction may not be shown for a junction with a minor side road

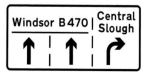

A sign that indicates the appropriate lanes to use for turning movements at a junction ahead is sometimes used in conjunction with, or instead of, a map-type or stack-type sign.

Route numbers in brackets are roads that will be reached by following the route indicated. Where a primary route is reached by following a non-primary route, its route number in brackets is shown on a small green patch. However, non-primary routes reached along primary routes are not indicated on white patches. "B1234" in the example is a non-primary route. Signs indicating a route to a motorway include a blue patch with the motorway number in brackets.

Flag-type sign indicating a primary route that leads to a motorway and to a non-primary route

Signs located at a junction and pointing along a road have chevrons rather than arrows. They are called "flag-type" signs. Some signs may be rectangular with upward-pointing arrows. These are used where the road divides, such as at an exit slip road or a forked junction. The background colour of a flag-type sign is that appropriate for the route indicated; coloured panels are not used where a primary route has a junction with a non-primary route. However, flag-type signs may include route number patches. A rectangular sign at the junction may have coloured panels, but only if it indicates more than one route.

Rectangular sign at a junction, indicating both a primary and a non-primary route. The background colour of the main sign is that appropriate for the main road on which the sign is located

Flag-type sign indicating a non-primary route

Rectangular sign at a junction, indicating a non-primary route

This sign indicates that a U-turn should be made at a roundabout ahead in order to follow the route to the destinations shown. It is normally located on a dual carriageway road.

Where a turning movement is prohibited, signs may show an alternative route.

Direction sign showing distances to destinations

A sign may indicate the distance to a destination in miles. Fractions of a mile may be shown for distances less than 3 miles. Signs may be provided after a junction listing destinations and distances: these are known as route confirmatory signs.

Route confirmatory sign

Route confirmatory sign including a regional destination (The SOUTH WEST) and the distance to a motorway

Route confirmatory sign: "Axtley" is on the current route; "Rickwell" is reached by turning onto the B 1555 at a junction ahead

Route confirmatory sign on a non-primary route leading to a primary route. "Lampton" is reached by turning onto the A 11 at a junction ahead

Some junctions on dual carriageway roads may be similar to those on motorways, where a slip road leaves the main carriageway via a deceleration lane or a lane drop. The first direction sign on the approach to the junction is usually located ½ mile in advance, although there may be an additional sign 1 mile before the junction. In some cases, these distances may be reduced, normally to ⅓ mile and ⅔ mile respectively. Another sign will be located where the deceleration lane starts or just before the left-hand lane leaves the main carriageway as a lane drop. The signs may be mounted at the side of the road or overhead.

Signs located at the side of the road where there is a deceleration lane. The number of lanes through the junction remains the same

Where the junction ahead is between two primary routes, any non-primary route at the same junction is not shown on a white panel. Signs on the exit slip road will have green backgrounds

The junction ahead is with a non-primary route only, with the destination shown in a white panel. The signs on the exit slip road will have white backgrounds

This sign is located at the start of the deceleration lane. In addition to the side destination, the sign shows the ahead destinations

Countdown markers indicate the distance to the start of the deceleration lane. Each bar represents about 100 yards. These signs may also be used on the approach to a roundabout or crossroads. On non-primary routes, the bars are black on a white background

A final route direction sign is usually located where the exit slip road separates from the main carriageway

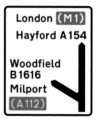

Signs on a non-primary route

Overhead signs for junctions with deceleration lanes and slip roads, where the number of lanes through the junction remains the same

| ↖ | (M 11 North) Lampton A 11 |
| ½ m | Longchurch B 1444 |

(M 11 South) London, Endsbury A 1 ↑

Primary route sign

½ m ↖ London A 4 Springwell, Foxley B 470

The WEST (A 4) Elkington, Hartcombe A 4207 ↑

Non-primary route sign

Signs for a junction where a lane leaves the main carriageway to become the exit slip road. Primary route signs have green backgrounds. Non-primary route signs have white backgrounds

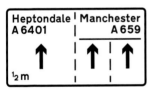

Matwell	London
A 222	A 2
↑	↑ ↑
½ m	

Axford A 37 ✔✔ London A 3
↑ ↑ ↑

Heptondale A 6401 | Manchester A 659
↑ | ↑ ↑
½ m

Signs mounted at the side of the carriageway in advance of the junction

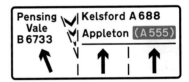

Pensing Vale B 6733 ✔✔ Kelsford A 688 | Appleton (A 555)
↖ ↑ ↑

Signs mounted at the side of the carriageway just before the left-hand lane leaves the main carriageway

Newark B 6180
▼

Leicester, Nottingham A 46
▼ ▼

Overhead signs

½ m

Springwell Foxley B 470
▼

Elkington Hartcombe A 4207
▼ ▼

Signs for tourist destinations

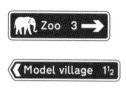

Tourist destinations may be shown on separate signs with brown backgrounds, or on brown panels incorporated into other direction signs. See page 84 for tourist destination signs on motorways.

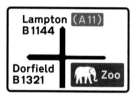

Symbols are often used to indicate the type of destination. These may be shown on road maps. Once the full name of a tourist

destination and its symbol have been shown on a sign, subsequent signs may show only the associated symbol. Examples of symbols are shown below.

Tourist information

Castle

Historic house

National Trust

English Heritage

Theme park

Country park

Bird garden

Nature reserve

Farm park

Safari park

Beach

Museum (England)

Roman remains

Aviation museum

100

There are also symbols for sports and leisure facilities.

Football
ground

Cricket
ground

Sports centre
(England)

Motor
sport

Golf
course

Race course

Fishing

Cycle hire

Ten-pin
bowling

Ski slope

See pages 103 and 104 for symbols and brown signs used for tourist facilities such as camp sites, restaurants and hotels. Some symbols are directional and face in the direction in which traffic turns at a junction. For ahead destinations, symbols generally face left. Some tourist attractions may use a general symbol, depending on whether they are in England, Scotland or Wales.

England

Scotland

Wales

This sign is used in advance of a junction, advising drivers of the route to be followed where it is not practicable to sign a tourist destination at the junction itself

Steam
railway
300 yds

Tourist
route to
Donford

Greenfields
Country Tour

Direction signs
may indicate a
route through
an area of
special interest

Archer Castle
10 miles

Signs showing the
distance ahead to
a tourist attraction

On the approach to a junction, a sign may indicate a town or geographical area with several tourist attractions.

Location of tourist information point or centre

Tourist information board (sign for pedestrians)

Direction to a tourist information point or centre

Direction to a parking place associated with a tourist attraction

Services signs

See page 86 for blue-background signs indicating motorway service areas located on all-purpose roads. Services grouped together at a single location on primary and non-primary routes may be signed where parking, toilets, fuel and refreshments are available at least between 8 am and 8 pm on every day except Christmas Day, Boxing Day and New Year's Day. Signs on non-primary routes have white backgrounds. Older signs on primary routes have green backgrounds, but are being replaced by white-background signs.

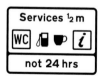

Distance to services

Direction to services

"not 24 hrs" may be varied to "Fuel only 24 hrs" or omitted if the services are open 24 hours every day. The cup symbol indicates that light refreshments are available. The wheelchair symbol denotes facilities for the disabled

102

The services may have a geographical name. The "LPG" symbol means LPG fuel is available, the spoon and fork symbol denotes a restaurant and the bed symbol indicates overnight accommodation. The lorry symbol indicates that the services are for goods vehicles only. Where the symbol has a red bar, services are not available for goods vehicles

Alternative signs indicating the entrance to services. May be used to indicate the direction to services at a road junction

Where individual facilities are available in a small town or village off the main route, signs at the junction indicate the direction in which they are located. If tourist facilities are available, the signs have a brown background and may include some of the symbols shown on pages 100 and 101.

Signs on the approach to the junction

Signs located where traffic turns at the junction

Brown signs may indicate establishments that provide restaurant facilities, light refreshments or overnight accommodation.

Licensed camping and caravan sites, youth hostels managed by the Youth Hostels Association or Scottish Youth Hostels Association, picnic areas, viewpoints and parking places with tourist information may also be indicated by brown signs.

Camping and caravan site: the tent or the caravan symbol may be omitted, depending on the facilities available. The name of the camp site may be shown

Youth hostel

Picnic area: may include a name

Distance to a parking place with toilets, tourist information, picnic area, telephone and viewpoint. The symbols may be varied as appropriate

Parking signs

Direction signs indicating parking places, such as off-street car parks, have white backgrounds, even on primary routes. Where the parking destination is incorporated into a primary route sign with a green background, it is shown on a white panel.

The signs may include various details about the parking places.

Where parking places in different directions are shown on a sign in advance of a junction, the "P" symbol may be shown at the top of the sign only

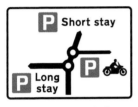

This map-type sign indicates the direction of routes to parking places from a double mini-roundabout ahead. The route to the right leads to a parking place for solo motor cycles only

A variable message sign may indicate the availability of spaces at each parking place. Some signs may show the number of vacant spaces; these are updated at regular intervals throughout the day

Where a parking place is for a particular class of vehicle, this may be shown by the appropriate symbol. This sign indicates a lorry park that is reached by making a U-turn at a roundabout ahead

Direction and distance to a multi-storey car park

Direction to a parking place that is available on certain days only

Direction to a parking place that has been approved by the police under the Safer Parking Scheme

Direction to a parking place showing the total number of spaces

Sign showing the facilities available at a parking place ahead. The lorry symbol is omitted where there is no restriction on the class of vehicle

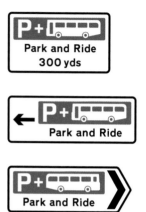

Signs may indicate the location of parking places associated with "Park and Ride" schemes. Where appropriate, the bus symbol is changed to another form of transport, e.g. tram, national railway or London Underground. The sign may include the name of the Park and Ride site or the place that it serves. It may also include the times of operation. Other direction signs may incorporate the blue "Park and Ride" panel.

Signs for drivers of goods vehicles

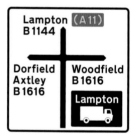

Routes recommended for goods vehicles have black signs with a white lorry symbol. Other direction signs may incorporate black lorry route panels. The most suitable route for lorries to a particular destination may be different from that for other vehicles. The lorry symbol faces in the direction in which vehicles turn at a junction. For ahead destinations, the symbol generally faces left. Where route numbers for motorways and primary routes are shown, these are placed on blue and green patches respectively.

Direction sign at a junction

Direction signs on the approach to a junction

This sign is used in advance of a junction, advising drivers of goods vehicles of the route to be followed where it is not practicable to sign the route at the junction itself

Signs for traffic diversions

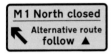

The symbol on this sign may be replaced by route numbers

Where, in an emergency, it is necessary to close a section of motorway or other main road to traffic, a temporary sign may advise drivers to follow a diversion route. To help drivers navigate the route, black symbols on yellow patches may be permanently displayed on existing direction signs, including motorway signs. On all-purpose roads, the symbols may be used on separate signs with yellow backgrounds.

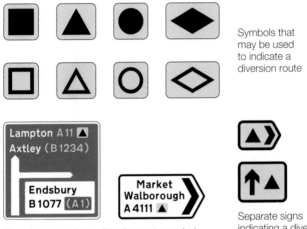

Symbols that may be used to indicate a diversion route

Signs incorporating a diversion route symbol that is shown alongside the road number of the route that drivers should follow

Separate signs indicating a diversion route (may be permanently displayed)

Temporary diversion signs may be required when a road is closed for reasons other than an emergency, e.g. to carry out works.

Examples of other direction signs

The name of the junction ahead may be shown at the top of the sign

Signs may incorporate hazard warning triangles. In this example there is an opening bridge on the road to the right

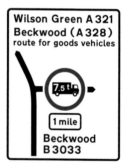

Signs may incorporate prohibitory roundels and indicate alternative routes

Direction signs at the junction may incorporate warning triangles or prohibitory roundels. A distance plate indicates that the hazard or restriction is not encountered immediately

A road through a by-passed town or village leads back to the main route

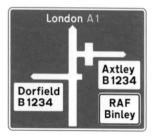

Staggered crossroads on a dual carriageway road: the white panel with the red border indicates a Ministry of Defence establishment

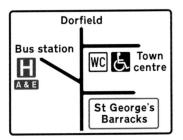

Ministry of Defence establishments may also be shown on separate signs with red borders, arrows and chevrons. The background colour is always white, even on a primary route

This sign shows a local road with three junctions ahead in close proximity. The "H" symbol on a red patch indicates a hospital with "A & E" facilities (if there is no "A & E", a blue patch is used). The "WC" and wheelchair symbols indicate toilets with facilities for disabled people

Local destinations, including a railway station and recycling centre, reached along a primary route

This sign shows both primary and local destinations that are reached along a primary route at a junction ahead. At some junctions, a separate sign might be used to indicate local destinations where this would avoid putting too much information on a single sign. In this example, the sign indicates that the primary route is a ring road

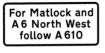

These signs are used where there are more destinations than can be accommodated on the signs at a junction. They are located in advance of the first sign for the junction and advise drivers of the routes to be followed for particular destinations

Signs may indicate an alternative route

Direction to an airport. The aircraft symbol usually points in the same direction as the arrow, as shown

Direction to a car ferry. The car symbols are replaced by the words "Pedestrian ferry" when the ferry is for foot passengers only

Direction to a vehicle ferry. The car symbol is replaced by a second lorry symbol when the ferry is for goods vehicles only

This primary route sign indicates the directions to a ferry and an airport. It also shows a road to which entry is prohibited

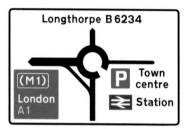

The route to the left has a priority lane that avoids the roundabout (see page 69 for road markings). The route to the right leads to town centre parking and a railway station

Direction to a London Underground station

Direction to a VOSA (Vehicle & Operator Services Agency) testing station for goods vehicles

Direction to a public telephone

Direction to public toilets with facilities for disabled people

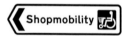

Direction to a "Shopmobility" service for disabled people

A modern version of the traditional fingerpost may be used at some junctions on minor rural roads. The sign may have a square end and may include a distance in miles. More than one destination may be shown

Signs indicating the direction to a new housing development may be left in place for up to six months after completion of the development

Signs with a light green background and yellow border are used to indicate the route for emergency vehicles to a permanent incident control point

Signs with a red background are used to indicate the route for emergency vehicles to a temporary incident control point

Signs that indicate the appropriate traffic lanes for turning movements at a junction ahead may be used alone or in addition to map-type or stack-type advance direction signs. Signs on primary routes have green backgrounds, and signs on non-primary routes have white backgrounds

These signs show how traffic lanes on a slip road join the main carriageway of a dual carriageway road at junctions. Signs on primary routes have green backgrounds, and signs on non-primary route have white backgrounds

Sign for drivers on slip road

Sign for drivers on main carriageway

The slip road joins the main carriageway as a lane gain to increase the number of lanes from two to three. A distance panel may be added

Sign for drivers on slip road

Sign for drivers on main carriageway

The right-hand lane of the slip road joins the main carriageway as a merge with an acceleration lane. This is followed by the left-hand lane, which joins the main carriageway as a lane gain. Chevron road markings normally separate the two lanes on the slip road. The distance may be omitted

Direction signs for cyclists and pedestrians

Direction signs specifically for cyclists have a blue background and include a white pedal cycle symbol. Most are free-standing signs, but some primary and non-primary route direction signs may incorporate a blue panel indicating a route for cyclists that is different from that for other traffic. The cycle symbol may also be used on pedestrian signs where cyclists and pedestrians share the route (see page 113).

Primary route direction sign, in advance of a junction, indicating a route for cyclists

Non-primary route direction sign, in advance of a junction, indicating a route for cyclists

Where the route indicated forms part of the National Cycle Network, the number of that route is shown on the signs in white numerals on a red patch. Links within the network may be designated as Regional Cycle Routes: signs indicating these have white route numbers on blue patches. Some local authorities may have their own numbered cycle routes using different coloured patches. Where a cycle route leads to a national or regional route, the number of the route to which it leads may be shown in brackets. Signs may also include the name of the route.

Number of a national cycle route

Number of a regional cycle route

Sign showing the direction and distances (in miles) to destinations along a named cycle route forming part of the National Cycle Network

Sign indicating two different cycle routes leading from a junction ahead

Direction of a national cycle route

This sign informs you that you are following a national cycle route with the number shown

Map-type signs may indicate the route through a junction. In this example, the sign shows the route across an entry slip road. A sign may be used to direct cyclists to a signal-controlled crossing

Signs indicating the direction to a parking place for pedal cycles

Direction signs for pedestrians generally have a blue background with white lettering and include the walking figure symbol. In town centres, especially pedestrianised areas, other colours may be used and the symbol may be omitted; these signs may also use different styles of lettering. Pedestrian routes to tourist attractions may have brown backgrounds and those for public footpaths green backgrounds. Signs may include distances in yards or miles.

Pedestrian and cycle route to a railway station

A public footpath may be indicated by a yellow waymarker. A blue arrow is used for public bridleways. The background may be of a different colour

Information signs

Information about the road ahead

Distance to the beginning of a dual carriageway road ahead

A section of dual carriageway road begins directly ahead

A short length of dual carriageway road begins directly ahead

Motorway

Primary route

Non-primary route

These signs indicate the loss of the right-hand lane on a dual carriageway road or one-way street. The signs may be reversed to indicate the loss of the left-hand lane. The number of ahead lanes is varied as appropriate. The signs are often used at the end of a climbing lane and may include a distance (as shown for the motorway sign)

No through road for vehicular traffic

"No through road" sign incorporated in a street nameplate

No through road for vehicular traffic in the direction indicated from junction ahead

This sign may be varied to indicate that a road is not suitable for a particular type of vehicle

Narrow road ahead with passing places at intervals

Passing place on a narrow road

Signs for lay-bys and parking areas

 Distance ahead to a parking place

 Location of parking place (may include an arrow to indicate the entrance to a parking area)

 Distance ahead to a parking place with an emergency telephone

 Location of parking place with an emergency telephone (may include an arrow)

 Distance ahead to a parking place for emergency use only

 Location of parking place for emergency use only (may include an arrow)

Boundary signs

Signs indicating county, town or village boundaries may include a crest or logo, a message of welcome, a phrase about a local geographical or historical feature, or the names of twin towns. They may be any shape or colour. The town and village signs may also include tourist attraction symbols and road safety messages. A speed limit sign may be placed in combination with a boundary sign at a village gateway (see page 76). Other signs may show the name of a river, inland waterway, bridge or tunnel.

Hospital signs

Hospitals with accident and emergency departments, or minor injury units, are indicated by red signs. The words "not 24 hrs" are omitted when facilities are available at all times

Blue signs indicate hospitals without accident and emergency facilities

The route to a hospital may be indicated on direction signs by the "H" symbol on a red or blue patch, denoting whether accident and emergency facilities are available or not (see page 109).

Signs for pedestrians

Stepped entrance to a subway

Ramped entrance to a subway

Ramped approach to a footbridge

Stepped approach to a footbridge

Direction to an emergency exit from a road tunnel

This sign advises pedestrians crossing the road that traffic is one-way in the direction shown

Signs for vehicle checks

Temporary signs are put out when vehicles are to be stopped for an excise licence check or vehicle inspection. These signs may apply to specific types of vehicle such as goods vehicles or buses, and they may indicate which lanes to use.

Examples of temporary signs for vehicle checks

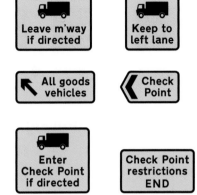

The type of vehicle indicated may be varied to a bus, or lorry and bus together

Police signs

These temporary signs are put out by the police to warn of potential danger or an accident ahead and the need to proceed with caution

In an emergency, drivers may be diverted onto the hard shoulder and told when to rejoin the main carriageway

Parking area reserved for police vehicles (the sign might say "Police vehicles only") or additionally, when varied to "Authorised vehicles only", vehicles such as those of the Highways Agency's Traffic Officers

Area where, from time to time, police carry out checks on the speed of vehicles

117

Signs for traffic surveys

These temporary signs are used when traffic surveys are taking place. Vehicles may be directed to stop at the census point

Other information signs

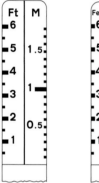 

The depth of water at a ford may be shown in both metric and imperial units, or in imperial units only

Signs used where there are separate entry and exit points to and from a car park, private access road or private property

Signs for drivers leaving the public road

Signs for drivers joining the public road

Emergency access
DO NOT OBSTRUCT

Where a road is physically closed part-way along its length to prevent its use by through traffic, this sign may be erected at the closure point. Vehicles should not be parked in a manner that would obstruct any gateway or opening that allows access for emergency vehicles

A temporary sign may be provided for up to three months following a permanent change to the road layout ahead. The sign may be varied to indicate the nature of the change, such as a new roundabout, or that the operation of traffic signals has been changed

Traffic signals

In most cases, in addition to the primary signals at the stop line, there are duplicate signals, known as secondary signals, located on the opposite side of the junction. If the primary signal is not working, you must obey the secondary signal as if it were the primary signal.

RED means **STOP**. Wait behind the stop line on the carriageway until **GREEN** shows

RED and **AMBER** also means **STOP**. Do not pass the stop line until **GREEN** shows

GREEN means go **IF THE WAY IS CLEAR**. Take extra care if you intend to turn left or right, and give way to pedestrians who are crossing

AMBER means **STOP**. You may go on only if the amber appears after you have crossed the stop line or are so close to it that to pull up might cause an accident

Signals indicating a right turn

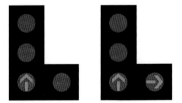

Although you may turn right on a full green signal, a right-turn **GREEN ARROW** showing at the same time indicates that turning right should be easier. Always check that opposing traffic has stopped before proceeding. If the full green is replaced by an ahead or left-turn arrow, you must wait until the right-turn arrow shows before you turn right

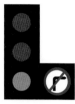

Signs may be placed with signals to qualify the meaning of the full green signal where movements through a junction are restricted

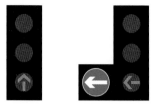

If movement is allowed in one direction only, the full green signal is normally replaced by a green arrow. This may be supplemented by a sign to reinforce the message

If a green arrow is shown with a red signal and the way is clear, you may go, but **only** in the direction shown by the arrow

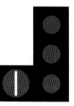

Additional white light signals may be provided for tram drivers (see page 31)

Light signals for the control of pedal cycles. **RED, AMBER** and **GREEN** have the same meaning as at normal traffic signals

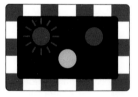

In addition to level crossings (see page 27), these signals may be used at other locations, such as lifting bridges, airfields or fire stations. When the **RED** lights are flashing you must stop. **AMBER** has the same meaning as at normal traffic signals

Tidal flow lane control signs and signals

On some busy roads, lane control signals are used to vary the number of lanes available to give priority to the main traffic flow.

| Lane control |
| 50 yds |
| → |

| Lane control |
| → |

Lane control on road leading from a junction ahead in the direction shown

| Lane control ahead |

| Lane control |
| 100 yards |

Lane control on road ahead

| Lane control on main road ahead |
| ↓ lane open |
| ✖ lane closed |
| ↙ move to left |

| Lane control signals ahead |
| ↓ lane open |
| ■ lane closed |
| ↙ move to left |

Special signs explain what the signals mean

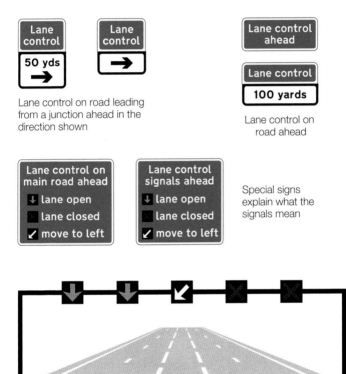

The lane control signals are displayed above the road to indicate the availability of the various lanes. A green arrow indicates that the lane is available to traffic facing the signal. A white diagonal arrow means that the lane is closed ahead and traffic should move to the next lane on the left. A red cross means that the lane is closed to traffic facing the signal

Alternative design of green arrow

Alternative design of white diagonal arrow

Alternative design of red cross

End of controlled section

Pedestrian, cycle and equestrian crossings

Zig-zag road markings

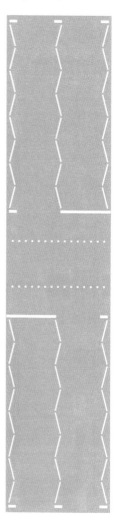

The zig-zag markings at crossings are there to ensure that drivers and pedestrians can see each other clearly. As a driver, you must not park your vehicle anywhere within these markings (before or after the crossing). Also, you must not overtake a moving motor vehicle within the zig-zag area before the crossing, nor must you overtake a vehicle that has stopped next to the crossing either to obey signals or because pedestrians are using a Zebra crossing (see page 127). If you are in a queue of vehicles that extends over a crossing, you should keep the crossing clear and look out for pedestrians who might be in the road. As a pedestrian, for your own safety, do not cross the road within the area marked by the zig-zags: keep to the crossing. Crossings for cyclists or horse riders also have zig-zag markings, and the above rules apply to these also.

Puffin crossings

The Puffin is the latest type of pedestrian crossing controlled by signals. It can detect the movement of pedestrians, so that it can give them enough time to cross safely and keep any delay to drivers to a minimum. The pedestrian crossing time is automatically varied according to the actual needs of the pedestrian and, if after the push button has been pressed the pedestrian decides to walk away, the call is automatically cancelled and the pedestrian phase will not appear. This avoids unnecessary delay to vehicular traffic and the irritation that might be caused by stopping vehicles when no pedestrians are waiting to cross.

For drivers approaching the crossing, the signals operate in the same manner as those shown on page 119: there is no flashing amber signal as used for the older Pelican crossing. If you are required to stop, do not proceed until you have a green signal and have checked carefully that the way is clear.

Near-side pedestrian signals with push button

The signals for pedestrians are located above the push button and are known as near-side signals. They can be seen when pedestrians are facing oncoming traffic. If the green walking figure is showing, you may cross the road, but take care in doing so. If the red standing figure is showing, press the push button and wait for the green figure to show. Unlike in older crossings, the green figure does not flash before the signals change back to red. If the red figure comes on when you are about to cross, press the push button and do not cross. Traffic will still be held on red for those pedestrians who are already crossing the road when the red figure comes on.

Toucan crossings

A Toucan crossing is used by both pedestrians and cyclists. Pedestrian and cycle signals are side by side and may be either near-side signals as for Puffin crossings, or located on the opposite side of the road (far-side signals). The signals for traffic travelling along the road (including pedal cycles) operate in the same manner as those for Puffin crossings (see page 123).

Near-side signals for
Toucan crossing

Cyclists who need to cross the road will be directed to a cycle facility off the main carriageway, adjacent to the waiting area for pedestrians. Near-side signals include red and green pedal cycle symbols, together with a call button for use by both pedestrians and cyclists. These signals operate in a similar manner to those for Puffin crossings. Far-side signals have both the green and red pedestrian signals, but only a green cycle signal. If the red standing figure is showing, either a pedestrian or cyclist should push the call button and wait until the green pedestrian and cycle signals show. Cyclists may ride across Toucans, whereas they should dismount at other crossings.

Far-side signals for
Toucan crossing

Push-button unit for
far-side signals

124

Equestrian crossings

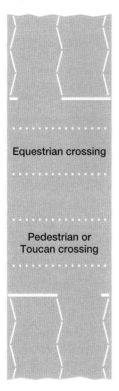

Equestrian crossing

Pedestrian or
Toucan crossing

These may be provided for horse riders where, for example, a public bridleway crosses a road. In most cases, there will be a parallel pedestrian or Toucan crossing. The signals for an equestrian crossing use the ridden horse symbol and may be either near-side or far-side. Operation of the crossing is similar to that of a Toucan crossing.

Far-side signals for
equestrian crossing

Near-side
signals for
equestrian
crossing

Push button
Wait for signal

Push-button unit for
far-side signals

Pelican crossings

Push-button unit

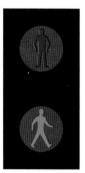

Far-side signals for
Pelican crossing

The Pelican is the older type of pedestrian crossing with far-side signals. It will eventually be replaced by the Puffin crossing described on page 123. At the end of the pedestrian phase, the green pedestrian signal flashes before the red standing figure

shows. At the same time, the red signal for vehicular traffic changes to a flashing amber signal (replacing the red and amber phase shown on page 119). The significance of these signals is that pedestrians should not start to cross, but should continue if already on the crossing; drivers may proceed, but only if the crossing is completely clear.

Signal-controlled junctions

Road junctions controlled by traffic signals may include crossing facilities for pedestrians, cyclists and equestrians. The signals may be either near-side or far-side. You should press the push button and wait for the green pedestrian, cycle or horse signal to show. Make sure that all traffic has stopped before crossing. Far-side signals for pedestrians operate differently from Pelican crossings. The green signal is followed by a blank signal: do not start to cross, but continue if you are already on the crossing.

Signalled crossings with central islands

Some signalled crossings may have central refuge islands. Where the crossings on each side of the island are in line, they operate as a single crossing. Where the crossings are staggered, they operate as two separate crossings.

Zebra crossings

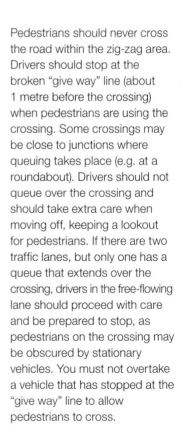

Pedestrians should never cross the road within the zig-zag area. Drivers should stop at the broken "give way" line (about 1 metre before the crossing) when pedestrians are using the crossing. Some crossings may be close to junctions where queuing takes place (e.g. at a roundabout). Drivers should not queue over the crossing and should take extra care when moving off, keeping a lookout for pedestrians. If there are two traffic lanes, but only one has a queue that extends over the crossing, drivers in the free-flowing lane should proceed with care and be prepared to stop, as pedestrians on the crossing may be obscured by stationary vehicles. You must not overtake a vehicle that has stopped at the "give way" line to allow pedestrians to cross.

Signs for road works and temporary situations

This sign, indicating road works or an obstruction in the carriageway ahead, may be used for any type of works, ranging from large construction schemes to minor maintenance

The "road works" sign may have a plate that indicates the distance to, the location of, or the nature of the works

End of road works and any associated temporary restrictions, including speed limits

Barriers are used to mark the boundaries of an area of the highway closed to vehicular and pedestrian traffic

At night or in poor daytime visibility, road danger lamps may additionally be used to indicate the limits of a temporary obstruction of the carriageway

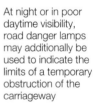

Traffic cones may be used to mark the edge of the route for vehicular or pedestrian traffic through or past a temporary obstruction

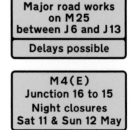

Signs may provide information about the location of current or future road works where delays or road closures are expected. This gives drivers the opportunity to allow more time for future journeys, use alternative routes, or make other arrangements for the duration of the works

On the approach to major road works, especially on motorways and dual carriageway roads, signs may indicate the nature and duration of the works

Signs for lane closures and contra-flow systems on motorways and dual carriageway roads

The traffic lanes that remain open are available to all traffic. The red bar indicates a lane that is closed ahead

Some traffic lanes that remain open may have restrictions. These signs show a narrow lane with a width restriction. Other restrictions may relate to vehicle height or weight

Traffic leaving at the next junction should use the near-side lane. This lane may also be used by traffic staying on the motorway

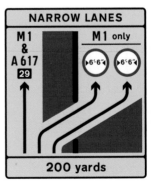

Traffic lanes divide ahead. The lane on the left leads to a junction and may also be used by traffic staying on the motorway. The right-hand lanes cross to the other carriageway. Areas closed to traffic are shown in red

Traffic lanes move across to the left, making use of the hard shoulder. Drivers are guided by temporary road markings or yellow road studs

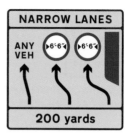

Traffic lanes ahead are narrower than usual and move towards the left. Vehicles exceeding the width indicated must use the left-hand lane

Two adjacent traffic lanes separate. The right-hand lane moves to the right, but remains within the same carriageway

Two traffic lanes move to the right: one crosses over to the other carriageway. The advised speed where the lanes divert is 30 mph

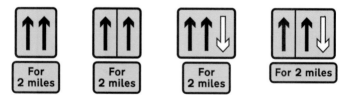

These signs show the distance over which the reduced number of lanes continue through the road works. The signs are repeated at regular intervals, usually every ½ mile. In these examples, there are no lane restrictions such as a width limit. The vertical black line indicates that the left-hand lane is the hard shoulder. The white downward-pointing arrow indicates a contra-flow traffic lane separated by traffic cylinders (see page 131). Where the contra-flow lane is separated by a physical barrier or a buffer lane (a lane closed to traffic), the white arrow is not shown

  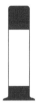

These repeater signs through the works are used where at least one lane has restricted use. The white downward-pointing arrow indicates a contra-flow traffic lane separated by traffic cylinders. Where the contra-flow lane is separated by a physical barrier or a buffer lane (a lane closed to traffic), the white arrow is not shown

Where a contra-flow system operates, traffic cylinders are used to separate opposing flows of traffic in adjacent lanes

Junctions may be accessible from within the road works area. The sign on the left shows an exit on the same carriageway. The sign on the right shows an exit reached from a contra-flow lane on the other carriageway. The style of numerals used for the route number depends on whether the signs are on a motorway or an all-purpose road. The black patch shows the motorway junction number

These signs are located where the exit route leaves the main through route. The upper sign is used on motorways and the lower sign on all-purpose roads

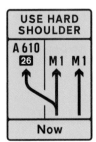

The hard shoulder is used as an exit lane at a junction

These signs show how lanes cross back from the opposite carriageway at the end of a contra-flow system

This sign indicates a lane change within the same carriageway. It is likely to be used near the end of the road works, prior to the carriageway being fully open

These signs indicate that use of the hard shoulder as a traffic lane has come to an end. Traffic is diverted onto the main carriageway. The sign on the right indicates that the carriageway ahead is fully open

Narrow traffic lanes revert to their normal width

Where delays are likely to occur at road works, the end sign may include a message of apology. The sign also means end of all temporary restrictions, including speed limits

This sign may follow the "end of road works" sign to provide a telephone contact number for the traffic authority responsible for the road works

Temporary signs indicating lane priority at junctions

Where slip roads leave and join at junctions within a road works site, the permanent arrangement for lane drop, lane gain and traffic merge may be temporarily changed. Signs may be provided to show the temporary arrangements.

Sign for drivers on slip road

Sign for drivers on main carriageway

The slip road joins the main carriageway as a lane gain to increase the number of lanes from two to three. The permanent layout might include a traffic merge with an acceleration lane. A distance panel may be added at the bottom of each sign

The slip road joins the main carriageway as a traffic merge with a "give way" line. The permanent situation would be a lane gain, as indicated by signs shown on pages 82 and 111. The distance may be omitted

Sign for drivers on slip road

Sign for drivers on main carriageway

This sign indicates a lane drop where the left-hand lane becomes the exit slip road. The permanent layout would be a lane diverge with a deceleration lane, with all three lanes continuing along the main carriageway

Signs for works traffic

Where it is necessary for works vehicles to gain entry to or exit from the works site itself, access may be directly from or to the open traffic lanes, such as a break in the line of cones. These entry and exit points are marked by red and white signs. Drivers should take care not to follow works vehicles into the site and to keep a lookout for vehicles leaving the site. These vehicles are likely to be moving more slowly than other traffic. Red and white signs may also be used to direct works traffic at road junctions.

Route to be used only by works traffic

Temporary access to a construction or road works site

Exit from a works site 200 yards ahead

Location of temporary exit from a construction or road works site

Works access on the left, 100 yards ahead

Sign to direct works traffic in advance of a road junction or works entrance

Sign to direct works traffic at a road junction or works entrance

Convoy working

At some road works, other than on motorways, it may be necessary to slow traffic to a speed of 10 mph. To ensure the safety of both road users and the workforce, traffic is taken through the works in convoy. At the start of the convoy section, traffic is controlled by either traffic signals or "STOP/GO" boards (see page 136). You must wait, where indicated, for the convoy vehicle that will escort you though the works. On single carriageway roads you must not overtake the convoy vehicle. On dual carriageway roads you may overtake the convoy vehicle, if it is safe to do so, after you have passed through the works area and signs have indicated that the speed limit has changed to a higher limit. Where traffic signals are used at the start of the convoy section, the red signal may show for a period longer than you would normally expect: **do not proceed until the green light shows**. Convoy working may take place at any time during the day or night.

Traffic signals ahead where convoy working is in operation

Advance warning may be given when delays are expected during overnight convoy working

Vehicles to be escorted in convoys through road works ahead

Reason for convoy working

Point beyond which vehicles should not proceed when temporary traffic signals show a red light

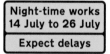

When the green light shows at temporary traffic signals, vehicular traffic must follow the vehicle escorting the traffic through the road works

Sign on convoy vehicle ("NO OVERTAKING" may be omitted)

Mobile road works and lane closures

Some road works can be carried out without the need for road closures or major traffic management schemes. The area of work is protected by a large stationary or slow-moving vehicle with a sign mounted on the back.

On single carriageway urban roads with a speed limit of 30 mph or less, the works will always be on the near side in the direction of travel. A "keep right" sign will be mounted on the back of the works vehicle or the vehicle protecting the works. There may also be a "keep left" sign on the front of the vehicle to be viewed by traffic travelling in the opposite direction. Additional static "road works ahead" signs may be placed at the side of the road and may include a distance plate such as "For 1 mile" or "Grass cutting for 1 mile". There may also be "road narrows on the left" signs (see page 11). The vehicle will usually have flashing lamps on its roof. The type of work likely to be carried out includes grass cutting, weed spraying and gully emptying. On some busy roads, traffic may also be controlled by "STOP/GO" boards (see page 136).

On single carriageway roads with a speed limit of 40 mph or more, the "keep right" sign on the back of the works vehicle or the vehicle protecting the works includes flashing amber lamps. These lamps flash in pairs from top to bottom.

On motorways and dual carriageway roads, mobile lane closures may be introduced on either the left-hand or right-hand side of the carriageway. More than one vehicle will be used to protect the lane closure. All signs will have flashing amber lamps. A light arrow may supplement the white-on-blue "keep right" or "keep left" arrow, and flash alternately with the amber lamps at the top.

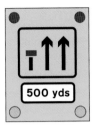

On the approach to mobile works on a motorway or dual carriageway road, vehicles with signs indicating the lanes that are closed will be on the hard shoulder or at the side of the carriageway. The type of work undertaken includes line painting, minor repairs and setting out static road works signs.

Mobile carriageway closures may be used to convoy traffic when it is necessary to hold traffic back while cones and signs are moved to change a temporary contra-flow system, or perhaps

to remove an overhead cable. All lanes on the carriageway will be closed, but traffic will move slowly forward, over a distance of several miles, on the approach to the area where the work is being undertaken. By the time the convoy reaches this area, the works should have been completed, traffic will be allowed to increase its speed and traffic lanes will be opened. The convoy vehicles will have a large red cross and red lamps flashing in vertical pairs.

Temporary traffic control

At some road works sites on single carriageway roads where two-way traffic flow is not possible, it is necessary to alternate the direction of flow by traffic control. This is known as shuttle working. For short lengths, this may be achieved by manually-operated "STOP/GO" boards at each end. At other sites, portable traffic signals will be used. They operate in the same way as permanent traffic signals (see page 119). Normally, a stop line is not marked on the road. A sign is used instead to indicate where you must stop when the red signal shows.

Temporary signals may be used to control a road junction. In this case, the red signal is likely to stay on longer than for normal shuttle working, as traffic on each leg of the junction will pass through the road works separately. There may be a junction within a length of road subject to shuttle working that is not controlled by signals. Signs will warn drivers of this.

Temporary signals control a junction. "3-way" may be varied to "4-way"

Signs for an uncontrolled junction on a road with shuttle working. The sign on the right is for traffic on the side road

Miscellaneous temporary signs

Details of a new road scheme under construction

Information about street works, with an emergency telephone number (sign for pedestrians)

Maximum speed advised, in miles per hour, on a road that has loose chippings

Maximum speed advised, in miles per hour, through road works

Temporary sudden change in level of carriageway

Sharp deviation of route to the left (right if chevrons reversed) at road works or other temporary obstruction

Where a mandatory speed limit is imposed at a road works site, advance warning may be given, especially on motorways and high-speed dual carriageway roads. However, this sign is less likely to be used in the future: the first speed limit sign will be located at the point where the speed limit commences

The end of a temporary mandatory speed limit is indicated by the "end of road works" sign (see pages 128 and 132). However, the message may be reinforced by a sign indicating the permanent speed limit beyond the road works. This may be combined with the "end of road works" sign. Where the permanent limit after the works is different from that in advance of the works, a speed limit sign is always used. The national speed limit sign shown in the example is varied to the appropriate limit

In the event of a breakdown within a road works site, await rescue by free recovery service

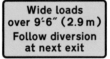

Instructions to drivers of wide loads on action to be taken before reaching road works ahead (instructions may vary)

Location of telephone to be used by drivers of wide loads to seek assistance

Additional traffic lane available ahead as part of a temporary traffic management scheme

Sharp bends ahead where traffic is diverted onto a temporary road for a short distance: the number of traffic lanes remains the same

This sign is used on a single carriageway road with more than two lanes, to indicate that a lane in the centre of the road is temporarily closed

Variable message sign ahead not in use or being tested

Traffic signals not in use

Zebra or signalled crossing facility temporarily out of use (sign for pedestrians, cyclists or equestrians)

Temporary sign used at road works to indicate the direction in which pedestrians should look for approaching traffic

Temporary route for pedestrians

Temporary sign used at road works to instruct cyclists to dismount and use the adjacent footway

Temporary hazard: vehicular traffic should proceed slowly

Vehicular traffic should proceed slowly, owing to workforce in the road ahead

Vehicular traffic must not proceed beyond the sign when it is displayed for a short period during works on or near a road (hand-held sign)

Hard shoulder temporarily closed for the distance shown

Temporary absence of road markings for the distance shown

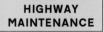

Sign on a vehicle being used in connection with highway maintenance works (flashing amber lamps are normally mounted on the roof of the vehicle)

Miscellaneous signs

HOV lanes

HOV lanes (**H**igh **O**ccupancy **V**ehicle lanes) are similar to bus lanes, but they can also be used by vehicles (other than lorries) with at least one passenger in addition to the driver, as indicated by the "2+" car symbol. Where the requirement is for at least two passengers in the vehicle, a "3+" car symbol is shown on the signs. Solo motorcycles are normally allowed to use HOV lanes, but large lorries are likely to be prohibited. Signs indicate which vehicles are permitted in the lane. The aims of a HOV lane are to reduce traffic congestion by maximising the use of a bus lane and encourage car sharing.

This sign gives advance warning of a HOV lane ahead

A separate sign gives the times of operation of a HOV lane ahead

Another sign indicates which vehicles may use the HOV lane ahead

Start of HOV lane (near-side)

HOV lane (near-side)

HOV lane road marking

End of HOV lane

HOV lanes (also known as car-sharing lanes) are to be introduced on some motorways. These could be on the right-hand side of the carriageway, where their use by buses might be prohibited. The HOV lane signs are likely to be mounted above the carriageway to indicate which types of vehicle may use, or are prohibited from using, particular traffic lanes.

Bus lanes

Signs and road markings for bus lanes are shown on pages 32 and 33. However, in recent years different types of bus lane have been introduced. These may be centre or right-hand lanes on the approaches to junctions, or may be lanes that can be used by other vehicles, such as solo motorcycles. Some examples are shown below. These signs may include a lower panel showing the times of operation.

Off-side, with-flow bus-only lane ahead (the bus symbol facing right indicates that the lane leads to a right turn at a junction ahead)

Near-side, with-flow bus lane ahead that can also be used by solo motorcycles, pedal cycles and taxis

Near-side, with-flow bus lane ahead that can also be used by lorries, pedal cycles and taxis

Off-side, with-flow bus-only lane leading to a right turn at a junction ahead

Near-side, with-flow bus lane that can also be used by solo motorcycles, pedal cycles and taxis

Near-side, with-flow bus lane that can also be used by lorries, pedal cycles and taxis

Road charging

Road charging was first introduced in central London and within a small area in Durham. The white on red "C" symbol is used on signs in both schemes and will, in future, be used to indicate road-charging schemes that might be introduced elsewhere. The symbol is not currently used for toll roads and tolled crossings, such as the M6 Toll motorway.

This example shows a typical zone entry sign. The charging period is shown in the lower panel. The name of the traffic authority may be shown at the top of the sign. The sign is usually supplemented by a "C" symbol road marking. Direction signs may incorporate the "C" symbol to indicate routes that lead into the charging zone. Details of the actual charges and the method of payment are available from the appropriate traffic authority.

Rising bollards

In some town and city centres, certain streets may be closed for part of the day, either to all traffic (e.g. pedestrian zones) or to through traffic, with access permitted, for example, to public transport. Enforcement of these restrictions may be by the use of automatic bollards that rise from the ground to provide a

physical closure. Where such bollards are in use, warning signs are normally provided. Where certain vehicles are allowed entry, red and green signals control the operation of the bollards. Only one vehicle should pass at any one time and may proceed only if the green signal is showing. Some vehicles, e.g. buses, have devices that can be recognised by detectors controlling the operation of

the bollards. If you are not driving an authorised vehicle, do not follow the vehicle in front, as you may risk personal injury and damage to your own vehicle. Where pedal cycles are exempt, a separate route avoiding the bollards is normally provided.

Rising bollards might also be used at the exit to a road-charging area, such as in Durham (see page 142). These operate when payment has been made (similar to the exit from some car parks).

Driver location signs

These have been introduced at regular intervals along many motorways and some other roads so that, in the event of a vehicle breakdown or other emergency, the exact location can be identified quickly. They show the motorway or road number, the carriageway identifier and a distance reference.

Variable signs

Some signs are designed to provide information about varying traffic conditions, such as delays or diversions ahead, or to warn of specific hazards, such as animals or debris in the road. These are called "variable message signs" and may be free-standing with an electronic display, such as the signs that have been erected above motorway hard shoulders. Some direction signs contain variable elements. They might show, for example, alternative routes, or the availability of spaces in car parks.

Signs activated by moving vehicles are provided as a road safety measure. They can give a reminder of the speed limit, or warning of a hazard such as a bend or crossroads. They are activated when a vehicle is travelling above a certain speed and the driver needs to slow down.

Variable signs are also used for traffic control, such as Active Traffic Management described on pages 91 to 93.

Acknowledgements

Photographs of the traffic signs on pages 4–8 (except p8 bottom) were taken by Simon Lusty of the Driving Standards Agency, with assistance from Graham Stanton, who kindly allowed the use of his "Roadside Heritage Collection" of historic signs.

Printed for The Stationery Office
J003309288   c300   04/17